A PLUME BOOK

TEN DISCOVERIES THAT REWROTE HISTORY

PATRICK HUNT is a global archaeologist who teaches on the faculty of Classics and Archaeology at Stanford University and has been the Director of the Stanford Alpine Archaeology Project since 1994. He also directs the National Geographic Society's Hannibal Expedition as the recipient of an Expedition Council Grant for 2007–2008. Hunt has been an elected Fellow of the Royal Geographical Society in London since 1989 and earned his Ph.D. at the Institute of Archaeology, UCL, University of London, in 1991. His research has been featured in *Archaeology* magazine and various international history and science magazines, and on the History Channel. He has written over one hundred articles and been published in over forty journals and encyclopedias and gives lectures on archaeology all around the world. He has broken at least twenty bones in falls from stone monuments during fieldwork, fought off kidnappers, avoided gunfire battles in guerilla warfare, and twice survived sunstroke-induced temporary blindness over the last twenty years in the pursuit of archaeology. This has not stopped him. He lives on the San Francisco peninsula in Northern California with his wife and spends several months a year abroad pursuing historical and archaeological research.

Also by Patrick Hunt

Caravaggio
Alpine Archaeology

TEN
DISCOVERIES
That
REWROTE
HISTORY

Patrick Hunt, Ph.D.

A PLUME BOOK

PLUME
Published by Penguin Group
Penguin Group (USA) Inc., 375 Hudson Street, New York, New York 10014, U.S.A. •
Penguin Group (Canada), 90 Eglinton Avenue East, Suite 700, Toronto, Ontario, Canada
M4P 2Y3 (a division of Pearson Penguin Canada Inc.) • Penguin Books Ltd., 80 Strand,
London WC2R 0RL, England • Penguin Ireland, 25 St. Stephen's Green, Dublin 2,
Ireland (a division of Penguin Books Ltd.) • Penguin Group (Australia), 250 Camberwell
Road, Camberwell, Victoria 3124, Australia (a division of Pearson Australia Group Pty.
Ltd.) • Penguin Books India Pvt. Ltd., 11 Community Centre, Panchsheel Park,
New Delhi – 110 017, India • Penguin Group (NZ), 67 Apollo Drive, Rosedale,
North Shore 0632, New Zealand (a division of Pearson New Zealand Ltd.)
• Penguin Books (South Africa) (Pty.) Ltd., 24 Sturdee Avenue, Rosebank,
Johannesburg 2196, South Africa

Penguin Books Ltd., Registered Offices: 80 Strand, London WC2R 0RL, England

First published by Plume, a member of Penguin Group (USA) Inc.

First Printing, October 2007
7 9 10 8 6

Copyright © Patrick Hunt, 2007
All rights reserved

Ⓟ REGISTERED TRADEMARK—MARCA REGISTRADA

LIBRARY OF CONGRESS CATALOGING-IN-PUBLICATION DATA
Hunt, Patrick.
Ten discoveries that rewrote history / Patrick Hunt.
p. cm
Includes bibliographical references.
ISBN 978-0-452-28877-5 (trade pbk.)
1. Archaeology—History. 2. Excavations (Archaeology)—History. 3. Antiquities.
4. Historic sites. 5. Extinct cities. 6. Tombs. 7. Civilization, Ancient. I. Title.

CC100.H86 2007
930.1—dc22
2007019808

Printed in the United States of America
Set in Granjon
Designed by Eve L. Kirch

This book is dedicated to my most keen fellow explorer,
my wife Pamela

Acknowledgments

This book proceeded out of my archaeological research over decades and a recent popular course at Stanford University. Archaeologists may not actually often rate the "Top Ten" sites or discoveries around the world, or make any such lists of most important sites, but it was an idea that seemed surprisingly obvious in terms of how much our understanding of ancient history is influenced by some relatively few but major discoveries. I felt it was vital for me to have some direct field experience at these sites or working knowledge of them. Admittedly, it is unusual for an archaeologist to range across so many cultures, regions and eras. The deliberate breadth-depth requisite of conducting archaeological research across five continents added years to my doctoral studies, and my Ph.D. dissertation (Institute of Archaeology, UCL, University of London) was not published in the usual single monograph form when finished back in 1991, but was instead split between at least seven different professional peer-reviewed academic journals. I am grateful to the Institute of Archaeology at London for allowing me such range.

This book would not have been possible without a patient, brilliant editor like Janie Fleming at Penguin/Plume, committed to publishing high-quality work and paying unflagging attention to detail. My literary agent, Carol Susan Roth—a writer's dream— immediately saw the potential to turn a global archaeologist's broad-ranging class into an accessible book.

I must credit Dr. Charlie Junkerman at Stanford, always visionary and prescient about what people are hungry to learn. My wife Pamela and daughters Hilary, Allegra and Beatrice were also equally supportive as we bounced around the world, sometimes bemused in Italy that the little Fiats we rented had no seat belts, but it would have been redundant anyway because our three girls were glued to their seats daily with wonderful and sticky gelato ice cream.

Friends who encouraged along the way include Chris and Teresa Hougie, Fritz and Beverly Maytag, Ed and Susan Catmull, Rob and Mary Anne Cook, Michael and Sande Marston and Bob Tousey. I am also deeply indebted to Helen and Peter Bing, Susan and Cordell Hull, and the National Geographic Society and its Expedition Council for sponsoring my archaeological research.

Contents

Introduction

How would archaeologists around the world list the most exciting and seminal global archaeological discoveries, events that "rewrote" history? Nearly every list would include some immediately recognizable discoveries such as King Tut's tomb, Machu Picchu, the Rosetta Stone, Troy, Pompeii, and the Dead Sea Scrolls, but would also include less familiar finds such as Akrotiri on the Aegean Island of Thera, China's Tomb of 10,000 Warriors, Nineveh and its Royal Assyrian Library of King Ashurbanipal, and the work of the Leakey family at Olduvai Gorge and elsewhere in the African Great Rift Zone. These are all excellent candidates for a global circle of discovery across many continents between 1750 and the end of the twentieth century.

Some of these discoveries were entirely accidental—for example, Pompeii, the Rosetta Stone, the Dead Sea Scrolls and even the Tomb of 10,000 Warriors. In some cases, amateurs first performed lengthy work, but eventually the discoveries all proceeded under professional archaeological teams. Other discoveries only culminated in triumph after hard years of persistent and logical searching, such as King Tut's tomb, Akrotiri on Thera, Nineveh, Olduvai Gorge and Machu Picchu. If we can accept Heinrich Schliemann's diaries and later accounts, which might be very risky, finding Troy might also fall in the latter category. Some of these discoveries were excavated first in the early days of archaeology, when treasure hunting was a more likely motive, and yet have continued for centuries as field models reflecting current archaeological philosophies and methods. Pompeii and Troy both fall into this category, as they continue to be studied up to the present. Other sites, including the Tomb of 10,000 Warriors, have been found fairly recently and only excavated within the past few decades. Sometimes politics and tourism make unlikely bedfellows with archaeological research, yet if increasing awareness of archaeological resources and commitment to protecting such cultural and historic resources results, this is probably a just end as well as a reasonable incentive to continue the search for human history.

This book examines each of these ten selected discoveries—whether deliberately sought or accidentally found—in the context of the evolving discipline of archaeology since the eighteenth century. Each chapter also briefly explores the intellectual, political and philosophical climate of the period when the discovery was made and evaluates it relative to the present. Although archaeology has changed greatly since 1750, it is questionable whether we should ever judge previous generations by our present values. What we understand and write about history has also changed greatly because of archaeology and the material cultures unearthed. How each of these events changed perceptions of history and the future directions of field research is also a considerable focus of this book. Subsequent generations of scholars may not agree over what are the most important archaeological discoveries of previous eras, but it is highly likely that these ten discoveries will stand out forever for archaeologists as well as for those who love ancient history and reading stories of discovery.

The precise accounts of the moment when each of these great discoveries was made differ somewhat. Some happened a century or more ago; others were unrecorded except by multiple spectators after the fact, each with different memories or observations; still others were written in often contradictory diaries by the same person. Although they are not overtly fictionalized, some of the first details of these discoveries can still only be guessed at. I have therefore tried to amalgamate the individual discovery details I consider most reliable. For this reason, any faults in reconstructing these discoveries or errors of detail in this book are entirely my own. Samuel Johnson once suggested that books record all we can know about history. But with all due respect, any decent archaeologist would choose to disagree, because the actual artifacts coming out of the ground may tell us far more than texts. Material history is at least as important as textual history and often foundational to it. That is why archaeology and its discoveries are so vital to understanding the past. When ancient texts are not enough or simply don't exist, this is when archaeology often rewrites history.

Chapter 1

Rosetta Stone
The Key to Egyptian History

Nile Delta, Egypt, 1799

It was 1799 and Napoleon's dream of a military and scientific campaign to the Nile had filled the desert with soldiers and the river with boat traffic. The intense heat of the Egyptian sun caused sweat to run down the necks of the French officers overseeing the local workers along the sluggish water's edge. This same water, once clear but now muddy, had traveled thousands of miles from the south, descending first through rapids in deep tropical Africa until it passed through almost lifeless deserts of sand and stone and finally slowed as it entered the Mediterranean in the delta. The French engineers were working on the defenses of their growing encampment, Fort-St.-Julien, on the west bank of an old port along the Nile, and to extend their fortifications along the water they had to tear down an old wall fairly close to it. The French had already had several battles with the Egyptians and needed to consolidate their power. They also had military intelligence that the British would likely be wanting to take Egypt for themselves, and they hoped this fort would deter the eventual British attack.

A French officer named Pierre Bouchard was supervising the workmen. He decided the unneeded dusty wall had been there a long time and was instructing the men to find the seams between the heavy stones for moving them. As they groaned and pulled, the wall finally tumbled and the individual stone slabs fell outward. Bouchard saw one large stone, about three feet long and a foot thick, land flat side up in a cloud of dust. It had one squared edge and the rest were broken. But what immediately caught his eye as the dust settled was that the face of this large flat stone was highly planed and totally covered with script, many lines of finely written text. He called for a halt to the workers and bent down to look closely. What he saw in the bright sun intrigued and then astonished him. He blinked his eyes to make sure. This stone, unlike so many other fragments of Old Egypt, had three distinct ancient scripts, each different. He had been in Egypt long enough to recognize the mysterious pictorial hieroglyphs of forgotten Egypt, but this top section—the most fragmentary—was followed by a section of language unrecognizable to him and then a far more familiar classical language text, with recognizable letters like *A*, *E*, *N* and what appeared to be an *H*, along with many other unfamiliar Greek letters.

Bouchard did not know that day that he had just discovered the world's most important key to decoding ancient Egyptian, but luckily he was curious and followed a hunch. Bouchard had his workers set the stone aside and set off to tell his superior officers. He must have been persistent going up the chain of command, because within an hour or so he reported it to his commander, General Abdallah-Jacques Menou. This extraordinary discovery would culminate a few decades later in the most exciting decipherment the world has ever known, that of the Rosetta Stone.

The discovery of "the stone" spread like wildfire among the French and, soon after, the British, who together helped decipher the text to give the world knowledge that had been lost for millennia. No credible historian or archaeologist, and certainly no Egyptologist worth reading, would argue with its importance. Decoding it, in the early 1820s, opened up ancient Egyptian language and texts—without it, the textual history of ancient Egypt would have remained locked away in forgotten history. Its triple script, sharing known with unknown language, also makes it the most important document in history. Yet, for all of its earth-shaking implications for revealing ancient history, it actually recorded a rather mundane event in the Egypt of its day. The stone's surprising discovery and sensational reception in Egypt caused an international tug-of-war for years between France and Britain, who not only fought over it diplomatically but also competed in deep scholarship to decode it. The exciting tale of its deciphering is a great detective story shared by two of the most important rival geniuses of the nineteenth century.

It's fair to ask where ancient historians would be without the Rosetta Stone. This one stone monument above all others changed the world, although no one would have known this when it was inscribed in 196 BC. Because its inscription was set down in several languages, the Rosetta Stone provided the key to understanding ancient Egyptian at a time when its meaning had been lost for almost two thousand years. Since 1822, only a few decades after it was found in the Nile and quickly translated by the polymath physicist-doctor Thomas Young (1773–1829) in England and the brilliant young Jean-François Champollion (1790–1832) in France, the Rosetta Stone has revolutionized our knowledge of the past.

Why is it called the Rosetta Stone?

The stone is called "Rosetta" after the place where it was found in 1799 in the Nile Delta, near the modern town of El-Rashid, where the French were building Fort-St.-Julien. In the wide and very flat Nile Delta, the great river forks into several branches before emptying into the Mediterranean. This particular one of its western branches has been called the Rosetta fork of the Nile River for centuries. But even though the name "Rosetta Stone" is firmly fixed in modern history, the Rosetta fork was not the stone's original home; it had earlier been moved there from an unknown location within Egypt.

The Rosetta Stone is incomplete because it was broken some-time in the past. At about three feet, nine inches long and two feet, five inches wide, it is now little more than two-thirds of its original size, just about five feet high. Originally it had a rounded top customary on a Ptolemaic stela (a small standing monument shaped like a grave headstone, only a little larger—an example is even shown on the last line of the Rosetta hieroglyph text). The remnant text—still enough to change ancient history—contains only fourteen of the likely twenty-nine hieroglyph lines, all of the thirty-two demotic lines (except for the top right-hand portion) and all of the fifty-four Greek lines (except for the bottom right-hand corner).

When was the Rosetta Stone carved and what was Egypt like at the time?

The Rosetta Stone dates to the Ptolemaic period in 196 BC, when Ptolemy V Epiphanes ruled Egypt. Actually more Greek than Egyptian, Ptolemy V was part of Alexander the Great's legacy from conquering Egypt along with the rest of the ancient world. Ptolemy V's ancestor Ptolemy I, after whom he was named, was a Macedonian, like Alexander himself. When Alexander died, worn out and sick, in 323 BC, Egypt quickly became the personal territory of Ptolemy I, one of Alexander's favorite companion generals, as the Mediterranean world was carved up between Alexander's lesser but still powerful successors. Ptolemy apparently even seized Alexander's sarcophagus en route to Greece and built a temple for its repose in order to legitimize his rule in Alexandria, the new city most exemplary of Alexander's ideals of unifying peoples. Displaying Alexander's trophy sarcophagus was a cunning public relations coup, especially because so many people still believed he was semidivine even when dead.

Alexandria was an amazingly vibrant hodgepodge of the old Egyptians mixed with Greeks, Macedonians, Africans, Semitic Asians and whoever else was attracted there by its cosmopolitan spirit soon after its founding. Greeks had been in Egypt for centuries, especially in the Nile Delta, trading and even writing Greek graffiti on old monuments and tombs. The first Greek colony in Egypt was Naukratis, founded at least four centuries before Alexander came along, but this new city of Alexandria was more than just a statement of conquest. It became synonymous with Alexander's ideals of blending of East and West in what would later be termed Hellenism. Although rarely lodged in Alexandria and too busy leading his armies in the East, Alexander devoted vast resources to the city. He wanted it to be one that would bring the world together, somehow uniting very different cultures. It would be a triumph of beauty in planning and architecture, its broad avenues lined with gleaming white marble colonnades and reflecting pools. Alexandria soon boasted the world's best library, the Library of Alexandria, and several temples serving a curious mix of religions that had elements of both old Egyptian and new Greek divinity and rituals. Because both the city of Alexandria and the Ptolemy conquerors were at least half Greek, Greek became one of the necessary spoken and written languages.

This biculturalism forced the old Egyptian priesthoods to either assimilate the Greek culture into their ancient religious system or die out. They chose survival and their scribes soon wrote Greek texts alongside the very traditional hieroglyphs, already thousands of years old, and the quick shorthand or cursive demotic text. These priests and scribes had even revolutionized ancient Egyptian hieroglyphs, making them more phonetic on a one-to-one exchange basis like the Greek alphabet, instead of a jumble of arcane combinations of ideograms, phonograms and rebus elements, although the Rosetta Stone's hieroglyphs are still a compendium of the former as well.

Details of the surprising text are not as important as their triplicity

Scribes for the hybridized Egyptian-Greek cults and state recorders serving several different constituencies of Egyptians and Greeks had to sometimes, although apparently not often, inscribe multilingual texts and decrees on stone to commemorate some event on the Alexandrian and Ptolemaic Egypt calendar. Why not write it in multiple languages so that the priests of both the Egyptian and the Greek temples could easily read it? We still do not know if the Rosetta Stone was a master text for less permanent, more perishable copies, or a single text unrecorded elsewhere. We do know that the hieroglyphs were translated from the Greek and not vice versa, and that the perhaps embarrassingly bureaucratic writing on this broken stone preserves the most mundane of texts. This is the background context to the Rosetta Stone, to this day the sole example of a triple language text from Egypt with sufficient detail to serve as the "key" to hieroglyphs.

The text on the Rosetta Stone is not as important as one might think; in fact, it is a rather mundane text called the Memphis Decree, which faithfully recorded details of the establishment of the royal cult as well as grain inventories and allotments. The nature of this decree was to help establish and confirm the royal cult of the boy king, Ptolemy V Epiphanes (205–180 BC). The stela or upright monument itself, probably 149 centimeters high before it was broken, has a traditional inscription dated to March 27, 196 BC. Thus the inscription records the decree when priests of Egypt formally put their strength behind Ptolemy, as he was only an adolescent of sixteen. The decree brought official backing for the king in a period of much unrest. In return for setting up a royal cult for the king, the priests would obtain favors from the king, including exemption from certain taxes. Thus the triple-script account on the Rosetta Stone is politically motivated.

Sharing known with unknown language makes it the most important document in history

Decoding ancient texts is a difficult task when there are few examples of the ancient writing to analyze and the language is a "dead" language not currently spoken. This is why, for example, our understanding of Minoan Linear A circa 1700 BC in Crete is still very tentative, because there just aren't enough texts to compare. It is the same for the famous stamped clay Phaistos Disc from Crete discovered in the early twentieth century, since only one example exists, and debate still rages as to its meaning. Even Mayan hieroglyphs from Central America are not completely understood, even though for the more recent Mayan scripts, from around AD 300 to 800, remnants exist today in indigenous modern dialects such as Tzotzil and Quiche. In comparison, the Coptic language script—a melange of ancient Greek and Old Egyptian—in modern Egypt has also existed for several millennia, although the older Egyptian remnants have had longer to disappear from modern Coptic, and finding them was not enough to help linguists reconstruct Old Egyptian.

This mix of so-called dead languages is what sets the Rosetta Stone apart: the very fact that it also contained a form of late ancient Ptolemaic Greek that could still be read—"dead but not forgotten"—gave linguists a known text to help translate an unknown text (Egyptian hieroglyphs) that was both "dead and forgotten." That it was inscribed also in triplicate form (Egyptian hieroglyph, Egyptian demotic and Ptolemaic Greek) made it even more valuable to decoding ancient Egyptian.

Decoding it has opened up ancient Egyptian language and texts

Being able to translate ancient Egyptian because of the Rosetta Stone has been a great boon to our knowledge of ancient history. In addition to viewing their art and monuments, we can now read their own Egyptian historians, decrees, religion, literature, science and medicine, technology and many other aspects of culture in their own language. We can see an artistic image and read the text that goes with it; we can "read" not only the physical structures and architecture but document the workforce that created them, since Egyptian records tell us such things as how many workmen, farmers, soldiers and stock animals were employed; and we can discover how many tons of stone and bushels of grain were produced. Taxation data, inventories and other administrative and economic data also provide us dates, reigns, contacts with other peoples and many other cultural events. Understanding ancient Egypt was impossible before 1822 when hieroglyphs could finally begin to be read again after almost two millennia. These forgotten historical data were only mysteries before Young and Champollion used the Rosetta Stone to decode the language of ancient Egypt. In other words, the whole culture has come alive since 1822 in ways that were previously unimaginable.

Its stone material has been misidentified for almost two centuries

Carol Andrews, for years a most valuable Egyptologist at the British Museum, used to joke that the great Wallis Budge, formidable keeper of the Egyptian Department at the museum in the late nineteenth and early twentieth centuries, would label things once and never change his mind. This is what happened to the Rosetta Stone, labeled by Budge as basalt stone when all the evidence was against it. Living in London, by 1987 I had spent much time in the famous museum and I knew it wasn't basalt. Carol Andrews often asked me questions about stone materials, as this was my doctoral research focus, and she was one of the first persons I told why it couldn't be basalt. My Ph.D. dissertation supervisor, Dr. Dafydd Griffiths, at the Institute of Archaeology a few blocks away, agreed with me. At a conference on archaeological stone in November 1991 at the British Museum, I was finally given permission by the guards to wedge myself underneath the Rosetta Stone, displayed at the time on a base off the floor. There I could see its underside had quartz vein intrusions as well as a grain structure that was closer to granitoid material than anything else. It clearly wasn't basalt. I showed this to other scholars at the conference, including Dietrich Klemm, considered an authority on Egyptian stone. Now the British Museum lists the material of the Rosetta Stone as granitoid, which is still an ambiguous category, but closer than basalt. Oddly enough, the original French records suggest it was something close to granite almost as far back as the original discovery, but perhaps Wallis Budge had not wanted to credit the French with anything!

It caused an international tug-of-war for years because its importance was immediately understood

As Brian Fagan has shown in *The Rape of the Nile*, Egypt was ripe for the taking around 1800 by European countries eager to establish collections from ancient empires. By 1799, Napoleon's French expedition had already removed hundreds of tons of Egyptian antiquities, storing them in Cairo before shipping them off to France. Some of this material would form the basis of a great collection in the Louvre Museum, including objects like the eight-foot-high black statue of a seated Rameses II and the fourteen-foot-long Great Sphinx of Tanis, not to mention hundreds of other images of ancient Egypt. Such was the spoil collected in Egypt by the French, and other continental powers would soon follow their example.

Upon seeing the Rosetta Stone, General Menou at El-Rashid immediately understood how important it was—he stored it in his own tent and had it cleaned. At El-Rashid, the Rosetta branch of the Nile, the stone was not in its original position when Bouchard's workers dug it out from the old wall. Because it had already been broken long since, it was clear it had been placed here much later, probably during or after the late Roman period in Egypt, around AD 500. The French tried to find other remaining fragments in the same river and port area in 1799, but they were unable to turn up any of the missing pieces, most likely because the original stone monument had been far removed from its original location even when originally broken. Even then any potential new fragments were considered "to be worth their weight in diamonds."

The French scholars in the expedition carefully studied the Rosetta Stone and verified that not only was the bottom text Greek from around 200 BC, but, as mentioned, the middle text was found to be demotic, an almost cursive, shorthand form of Late Egyptian. Demotic was often used as an administrative language in tandem with Greek in Late Egypt at the time of the Ptolemies, circa 200 BC. The Rosetta Stone was taken to Cairo and placed under the curation of the French Institute of Egypt, where scores of French visitors hurried to view it, both scholars and military officers alike. Back in Egypt the stone was being used as a sort of printing plate, like a lithograph, inked and copied for distribution. A French newspaper, *Courier d'Egypte*, even announced its discovery in late 1799 as a possible "key to hieroglyphs," and by fall of 1800 the scholars of the French Academy in Paris found that some knowledge about the Rosetta Stone had even reached the general populace there.

News of the discovery spread rapidly in French and soon British circles. What the French had feared about British intentions was soon to be realized. When the British successfully blockaded and defeated the French in Egypt in 1801, the Rosetta Stone was already one of the objects central to negotiations in turning over France's recently acquired Egyptian antiquities to the new British conquerors. General Menou could have protected the Rosetta Stone by sending it out of Cairo to France earlier, but instead he'd had it transported to Alexandria, possibly because he secretly considered it his personal property. Menou was not on good terms with the scholars of the French Institute of Egypt and when the threat of British forces began to materialize in the blockade of the Nile, he retreated to Alexandria with the Rosetta Stone in his possession. The earlier chance of shipping it to France with the rest of the Egyptian antiquities was now lost, but Menou had probably delayed in anguish, knowing that if he sent it back to France he would have lost any control over it. The few scholars left in his entourage became the Rosetta Stone's temporary curators, under his watchful eye, and they wrapped it in packing to hide it from the British forces who were overrunning Egypt. The retreating Napoleonic French expedition were doing their best to evacuate Egypt with whatever they could keep from the British but now General Menou had waited too long.

The British must have had spies in shipping because they knew the Rosetta Stone had not left Egypt. From the highest British orders on down, the mandate was to obtain the Rosetta Stone at all costs. As spoils of war, the British general John Hutchinson required all antiquities to be turned over for his safekeeping. Negotiations for the British in 1800 were conducted by a clergyman, Edward Clarke, and the diplomat-collector Sir William Hamilton. The British had tracked the Rosetta Stone directly to General Menou. In his book *Cracking Codes*, Richard Parkinson relates the anecdote that upon being forced to give up the Rosetta Stone, General Menou could be heard bellowing from his tent, "Never has the world been so pillaged!" This apparently amused the British because to them Menou was the epitome of an official looter.

The French, especially General Menou both as an individual but also now suddenly representing his country in protest, were understandably very upset to part with it as the Rosetta Stone had already become a French national treasure, not because of anything aesthetic but because of its triple language texts, whose significance, if not meaning, was already clear. The Rosetta Stone would remain a focal point in nationalistic competition over Egyptian matters between the French and British for decades, revived in the decoding race of the Rosetta Stone by Champollion and Young, rivals whose roles have been promoted or downplayed by both French and British historians.

The tale of its deciphering is a great detective story shared by rival geniuses

The Rosetta Stone was firmly ensconced in the British Museum by 1802 in a royal decree by George III, but its casts and rubbings, some of them taken back in 1800 in Egypt, proliferated in collections such as the Vatican's and in centers of European learning including Uppsala and Leiden and even Philadelphia's Philosophical Society, where academicians and scholars tried (unsuccessfully for the most part) to make sense of the hieroglyphs. In the next few years, several linguists who could already read the Greek were able to make some headway in translation. Among them were the Orientalist and linguist Baron Silvestre de Sacy, who was able to decipher the demotic name for Ptolemy, and the Swedish scholar J. H. Ackerblad in 1802, neither of whom receive sufficient credit for their linguistic advances in reading hieroglyphs.

The main figure in this almost mythic story is usually Jean-François Champollion (1790–1832), who had already learned eight languages, including Hebrew, Greek and Latin, by age sixteen. He was held in such high esteem even before publishing his Rosetta Stone studies in 1822 that he became a professor at the Lycée of Grenoble at age nineteen. The other figure of at least equal brilliance is Thomas Young (1773–1829), a British medical doctor, linguist and physicist of optics who was one of the first in modern times to formulate and use logical principles of what would become cryptography. Like Champollion, Young had mastered at least seven languages as an adolescent, and he was widely regarded as a genius scientist and universal scholar (called "Phenomenon Young") and Champollion a genius linguist. Neither Champollion nor Young was working directly with the Rosetta Stone but instead with copies. The fact that one man was French and the other British heightened the nationalistic tension and competition in this race to decode the Rosetta Stone. Most likely because France could never forgive Britain for taking the Rosetta Stone from them by force after French discovery, French historians to this day usually mention only their countryman Champollion in the decipherment and are very grudging about giving the British scientist Young any of the credit that he is rightly due.

Champollion's older brother Jacques Joseph Champollion-Figeac (1778–1867), a professor of Greek at the University of Grenoble, had much earlier, in 1802, encouraged twelve-year-old Jean-François to study the inscription of the Rosetta Stone if he wanted to make a lasting mark on Egyptology. Jean-François eventually became a student of Silvestre de Sacy at the College de France in Paris and there he learned Coptic, the latest ancient version of Egyptian (using mostly Greek letters) surviving from the Roman period. Under de Sacy's tutelage, at age sixteen in 1806, the brilliant young Jean-François Champollion gave a paper to the Society of Sciences and Arts in Grenoble showing that Coptic was a remnant of Old Egyptian and the last language of Old Egypt. Thus Champollion gradually homed in on the old hieroglyphic language of Egypt over the course of at least a decade. Champollion was almost fanatically supportive of Napoleon in his political outlook, so it was no surprise that Napoleon signed the official paperwork making Champollion a doctor in 1809, which was an unusual elevation outside of and above the normal academic bureaucracy.

In 1814, when he was twenty-four, Champollion wanted to have a better copy of the Rosetta Stone "lithograph" since his older sources, taken from the earliest French and British copies of its text, did not quite match up. He began correspondence with the brilliant Thomas Young, who was forty-one years old, seventeen years his senior, and served as the foreign secretary to the Royal Society. Champollion requested verification of certain passages. The usually generous Young quickly obliged but with not much more than was necessary.

In 1815, Baron de Sacy warned Thomas Young against his former student Champollion in a letter, suggesting that Young should guard his original research more carefully, saying:

I think, Monsieur, that you are further ahead [than Champollion] and that you can read a considerable part of the Egyptian hieroglyphic text. But if I had one piece of advice to give you, it would be to not communicate your discoveries too much to M. Champollion. It could transpire that he might then claim to have been first.

Such was the continuing intense rivalry between France and Britain over Egyptian antiquarian interests, no doubt in part fueled by that French resentment over having lost the Rosetta Stone, widely popularized as the "key" to Egyptian hieroglyphs.

By 1816 Thomas Young had long recognized the importance of the cartouche "envelope" seen around Egyptian royal names and had correctly translated the cartouche-enclosed name of Ptolemy in the hieroglyph portion of the text and accurately recognized sound signs for *p*, *t*, *i*, *s* and *m*, among others. Young's credit, however, was acquired in Britain mostly after his death.

After Napoleon's 1815 defeat at Waterloo and exile to Elba, Champollion continued his unpopular public support for Napoleon and lost his professorship at Grenoble in 1821. His brother Jacques Joseph came to his rescue, and Champollion went to Paris to live under his brother's roof.

In 1819 Thomas Young published his translations of the names for Ptolemy and Cleopatra in *A Supplement to the Encyclopaedia Britannica*, which most British (but not French) historians of Egyptian linguistics maintain Champollion soon read and annotated with his own ideas.

On September 14, 1822, Champollion received and read long-awaited and detailed reports of hieroglyphs at Abu Simbel, sent from a friend on his travels in Egypt. These included inscriptions for Rameses II and the god Thoth as well as others with Pharaoh Thutmose III. His sequence of deductions went something like this, although there is still a great deal of debate about the reconstructed events: By comparing them with copies of the Rosetta Stone text, Champollion could verify and reestablish some of the phonetic signs that Thomas Young had already suggested. These included excellent logical guesses for Ptolemaic variants of *k*, *l*, *m*, *p*, *r*, *s* and *t*, several of which were shared (*l*, *p*, *t*, *r*) between the royal cartouches (elliptical "braided" envelopes around names) for the names Ptolemy and Cleopatra. Champollion then saw a sun disc symbol as representing the god Ra and followed by a double *s*. He correctly deduced that the symbol in between the Ra and the *ss* must be an *m* sound. He verified this by examining an ibis symbol for the god Thoth, which was combined with a similar *m* plus *s*, establishing his primary breakthrough in a table of Egyptian phonetic sounds. Champollion was fortunate that Ptolemaic Egyptian had added some vowels to translate Greek equivalents, where earlier Egyptian did not use vowels. Champollion's achievement—not unaided—was that he showed Egyptian could now be proven to contain some phonetic alphabet letter equivalents as well as readable nonphonetic symbols, now called logograms, the latter working like a rebus. A rebus is a combination of ideas, often abbreviated visually and phonetically. For example, modern symbols combining pictures for an eye and a heart and the letter *U* can be read as an English rebus for "I love you." Without doubt it was the Rosetta Stone itself with its triple ancient language texts that provided the comparative linguistic framework and impetus for both Young's and Champollion's research. Public interest in this famous stone must have certainly attracted other researchers, such as Silvestre de Sacy, Johann Akerblad, and Stephen Weston, to its text again and again and likely whetted their scholarly appetites and linguistic abilities for its decipherment. Soon enough, Champollion could finally confirm his new hieroglyph assessments, the mathematician Young's research having paved the way for years with so many logical tips and linguistic directions.

Legend says Champollion went running to his brother's office at the institute and shouted "I've done it!" The Champollion myth also says he collapsed for five days from his mental exertions, but this is likely a Romantic invention. Champollion's older brother now had access to the French Institute for Inscriptions and Belles Lettres as secretary to one of its chief officers, Baron Joseph Dacier. To immediately publish his findings, Champollion wrote his famous *Letter to M. Dacier* over the next few days, yet cautiously backdated it to September 22, probably for fear of being upstaged. This backdating seems to many

British historians to be evidence of guilt over an unacknowl-
edged debt to Thomas Young. But there in his official document
Champollion explained his seemingly individual discoveries and
solutions for Egyptian hieroglyphs with tables of phonetic read-
ings. Almost a week later he read this document in Paris before
the entire assembly of the French Institute.

The results were received with near spontaneous praise and
wonder in Paris and soon after across all of Europe. Now a
national hero for beating the British to the discovery, Champollion was universally hailed as a genius (which was true, after all)
and the sole antiquarian linguist who had solved the mystery
of ancient Egyptian hieroglyphs (not true), whose meaning had
been lost to the world of history for almost two millennia. Apparently Champollion's address did not once credit anyone else,
certainly not his British rival Thomas Young, whose years of
careful work he had built upon without acknowledging his debt.
What is not often recorded is that Thomas Young was in that
very audience on that day, September 27, when Champollion
read his report to thunderous acclaim. Without too much bitter-
ness, Thomas Young wrote this subtly revealing letter to Sir
William Hamilton, the most famous collector of antiquities of his
generation:

> I have found here . . . M. Champollion, junior, who has been
> living for these ten years on the Inscription of Rosetta . . . It
> may be said that he found the key in England, which has
> opened the gate for him . . . You will easily believe that were
> I ever so much the victim of the bad passions, I should feel
> nothing but exultation at Mr. Champollion's success.

Perhaps oddly, the off-and-on correspondence between Champollion and Young continued until 1829 when Young died,

generous with his research to the end. Champollion went on to become a chief officer of the Louvre Museum in 1826. Finally traveling to Egypt in 1828–29, he died in 1832 at age forty-one, having received, through to this day, the lion's share of fame for decoding the Rosetta Stone.

Conclusion

The Rosetta Stone connects ancient Egypt to the Ptolemaic period and is without question our link to a forgotten language. As Egyptologist J. G. Manning recently (2007) wrote to me in response to my question about his view of its importance:

> The fortuitous discovery of the Rosetta Stone, and Champollion's brilliant and groundbreaking work on the texts recorded thereon, opened up Egyptian civilization in its own terms for the first time. Simultaneously, and equally importantly, it shed important light on the relationship between the Ptolemaic kings and the Egyptian priests in an epoch when Egypt's ancient past was being reinvigorated. The Rosetta Stone is, at once then, the foundation text of Egyptology and a crucial link between ancient Egypt and its legacy to the modern world.

Seven years after Champollion's momentous Paris event in 1822, Thomas Young died in 1829 in his mid-fifties without public acknowledgment of his huge role in deciphering the Rosetta Stone, remembered and honored instead in his lifetime and beyond for his scientific genius. Young was even elected to the French Academy of Sciences in 1827 as one of only eight foreigners, but ironically it was for Young's accomplishments in the sciences and not for his decoding work on the Rosetta

Stone and deciphering of Egyptian hieroglyphics. Even if we can never fully properly credit Young and Champollion and their predecessors equally, that our understanding of the world of ancient Egypt was forever changed after the Rosetta Stone is without question.

Chapter 2

Troy

The Key to Homer and Greek History

Hisarlik, Turkey, 1870

Holding a favorite book in one hand, Heinrich Schliemann stood on the windy hill, facing north in the breeze off the sea. His eyes could just barely pick out the far sliver of water as the setting sun glinted off it. He looked down at his text. It was the *Iliad*, Homer's great epic poem about Troy. Schliemann's fingers moved down the text to where he could read about the streams of the Simois and the Scamander running to the sea. He looked up again and his eyes then traced along the valley below, just the kind of terrain where such rivers could have meandered thousands of years before. He calculated the distance to the sea and thought it was just about right, imagining Greek warships once landing where a bay might have been long ago, now filled up with silt. Then he pivoted around on his boot and turned south, straining his eyes in the distance to find the last light of the day glowing on a mountain that would have been easily visible for any people living on this hill so long ago.

His eyes dropped back down to his text, and he searched for the passage about Mount Ida in Homer, mentioned in the poem as being to the south of Troy. The poem and the landscape in which he stood really did match, he realized. Noticing something for the first time, he stooped down and picked up an old broken piece of pottery, thick and worn. Turning it over in his hand, he wondered how long ago the complete pot had held water, grain or olive oil. With his boot he kicked at the soil beneath him, and dusk settled in, but not before he had brought to the surface several other potsherds. None of the broken pottery matched, he noted in the growing dimness. But this was a good sign, suggesting there must be a lot of broken pottery beneath his boots. Clearly a lot of pottery meant a substantial settlement of people had lived here at one time. His mind racing, Heinrich Schliemann wondered if this really could be Troy. Putting the broken potsherds in his coat pocket, he walked down the hill, vowing to return in the morning with some tools and baskets. He began to believe that Homer's details about the fortress of Troy perfectly matched this old hill. He could almost hear the cries of battle in his imagination, one strong voice belonging to the mighty Greek hero Achilles. . . . Whether or not this story is true, Schliemann was right that Troy existed.

The destruction of Troy

The hilly streets ran with blood and the night air was filled with the clashing of swords and shields and the cries of people as doors were battered down. Everywhere was the choking smell of fires burning. The high and broad walls of massive stone were intact, but the wooden gates were breached. The bright flames could be seen for miles over the blackened silhouettes of falling towers, and a thick column of smoke billowed above the proud fortress city that guarded these hills and valleys where two continents came together. If people could flee, they went eastward and southward away from the marauders whose ships were beached not far below the hill. The smoke was visible for miles as mighty Troy was destroyed.

After hauling the bloodied surviving men and weeping women away into slavery, the looted city would be abandoned for centuries. Erosion of the upper mud brick walls, dissolving into indistinguishable soil, would eventually affect most of the remaining walls. Wind-driven seeds would grow in the ash and soon new grasses would cover the softening hill, waving in the wind from the sea. Then native shrubs would grow back over the bits of stone foundations and finally trees would make the landscape no different from any other in the region. If an eagle or seabird landed on the wooded hill a few generations later, it would detect almost no trace of its great past. The birds would not hear echoes where battle cries once rang out, or before that the songs of children, the banter of merchants and the decrees of kings and queens. Only silence would reign at Troy for a long time.

We are fairly able to reconstruct this event or one like it; this is not just the subject of poetry and myth but, in fact, the closing hours of a great civilization that came crashing down around 1200 to 1100 BC. Whether there was one war or a series of many smaller battles, whether the cities were invaded from the outside or collapsing from within, this story became legend. This legend was repeated at Mycenae, Thebes, Tiryns and many other fortress cities of the Late Bronze Age in and around Greece when order descended into chaos and the Dark Ages fell upon Greece for hundreds of years. In that intervening period, the time of heroes and the legend of Troy was not forgotten but the language changed greatly. The new way of writing its sounds was altogether different; instead of the old method of inscribing a picture-based type in the Late Bronze Age (ending around 1100 BC), as seen on clay tablets found at many of the old sites like Knossos and Pylos, the new writing form used an alphabet borrowed from the Phoenician traders after 900 BC. What had been written in the old form is now called Linear B and is identified as a Mycenaean-style text. Now we know that Linear B was essentially an early form of Greek. Both the language and the new way of writing it as an alphabet changed in the transition of civilizations.

But these new Greeks remembered the stories that were handed down from parent to child, from poets reciting by the hearths to audiences eager to hear of past glories. The story of Troy was a fabled one they all knew from being told many times over. No doubt the rapt listeners could anticipate some familiar words and phrases and even appreciate the poets' innovations about once-great Troy.

Since the nineteenth century, Troy has been transformed from myth into history. While stories about Troy and the Trojan War have dominated the Western imagination for millennia, they also inspired the foundation of modern archaeology. Every new generation peering back through time at Troy seems to need to ask: Why is Troy and its discovery so important? The rediscovery of Troy helped establish modern archaeology, as matching Homer's epic poem to the landscape set precedents for other discoveries along the same method of matching texts to topographies. In fact, Troy was not just a place connected to the Bronze Age epics; it had many layers of civilization, stretching over thousands of years. The first excavator at Troy, Heinrich Schliemann, amazed the world with startling showmanship and a knack for media manipulation, but, however questionable his motives and methods, he persuaded the world that Troy had really existed. Troy serves as a good example of a kernel of historical truth embedded in myth. One of the core myths of Troy, the Trojan War, would not have happened because of a beautiful woman like Helen, but would more likely have been a territorial battle over trade rights. Another core myth, the Trojan Horse, also has historical roots in the westward migration of horses and their first arrival in the Mediterranean world from the central Asian steppe lands. Troy was also known outside Greece; texts from the Bronze Age Hittites, a prominent culture of ancient Turkey, show they knew the place, also called Ilion, as Wilusa. This proves Troy's existence at that time. Long after Schliemann did his initial work at Hisarlik, Turkey, renewed modern excavations at Troy continue to demonstrate its importance.

On the hill of ruined Troy in 480 BC, the Persian emperor Xerxes ordered the sacrifice of a thousand cows before setting out to attempt to conquer Greece, affirming Homer's legends that this site marked the age-old conflict between Asia and Europe. After conquering Constantinople in 1453, Sultan Mehmet II rode his horse up the then mostly bare hill at Hisarlik, Turkey, again marking the site for Asia instead of Europe. This is in contrast to Homer's poem where the Greeks burn Troy, then called Ilion. As late as 1453, people knew this was the site of ancient Troy. But after the Byzantine world was conquered and Constantinople became Istanbul, the historical Troy was replaced by the Troy of myth. Indeed, by four hundred years later, when Schliemann made his discovery, Troy had been relegated to myth, and very few believed it had even existed except in the imagination of Homer and his Greek heirs.

The rediscovery of Troy helped establish modern archaeology

Before 1872, the majority of European scholarship treated Troy solely as the subject of an epic poem, certainly among the world's greatest, but a place unlikely to exist outside its mythological subject. Poetry after all could hardly be expected to be historical, regardless of how many people could recite many lines from Homer by heart from their school days. Evoking the names of heroes like Achilles, Odysseus and Hector was merely a literary pastime; no one tried to assert in the early nineteenth century that these legendary figures existed. The same judgment was made about Troy, immortalized again much later than Homer in Christopher Marlowe's lines about Helen: "Was this the face that launch'd a thousand ships / and burnt the topless towers of Ilium?" Furthermore, archaeology as we know it now was not an academic discipline taught in the great European universities. Archaeology was still in its infancy and consigned mostly to treasure hunting for antique sculptures to adorn the great houses of Europe as a romantic reminder of ancient times.

While we can trace the Western ideas of archaeology back to the ancient Greeks—a historian named Idomeneus in the third century BC wrote about "ancient words" (*archaiou logou*)—it was apparently mostly about the study of old languages. The very definition of the word *archaeology* has greatly changed in the last few hundred years.

The first great English dictionary writer, Samuel Johnson, suggested around 1755 that books record all we can know about history, expressing no perception about what of the past could be recorded through physical remains. *Archaeology* was then defined as what could be gleaned about general ancient history from texts, and it was only gradually expanded over the next century to include the study of material remains. Troy's role in that changing perception should not be underestimated. According to the *Oxford English Dictionary*, one of the first uses of the word *archaeology* in English occurs in 1607 with "*archaiology* of the Jews," but it was mostly about texts and general antiquity. By 1872 the dictionary said, "*Archaeology* displays old structures and buried relics of the remote past." This evolution of the word is confirmed by 1880, after Troy's seminal excavations, when we read, "The archaeologists have raised the study of antiquities to the level of a science." Suddenly with Troy—where Heinrich Schliemann was searching for an ancient lost city—and related methodological excavations, there was a huge watershed change. Archaeology became both a merging and redividing of the old discipline of ancient history, reading ancient texts, and the new discipline, "reading" what was in the very ground. Now the ancient materials themselves, the buried past, formed the new focus of archaeology.

By approaching Troy and other ancient places in a new way, pioneering archaeologists set about proving hypotheses that a given ancient city existed rather than just plundering a site for its antiquities. In this way Troy served a higher purpose: it was necessary to engage the skeptical academic world with material evidence. Schliemann is surrounded by a swirl of controversy today, not the least of the charges being that he might have fabricated the so-called Treasure of Priam or salted the site with modern or reworked artifacts. But what is often forgotten is that he heralded a whole new era, in which material artifacts buried for millennia have a story to tell. In Schliemann's case, his version of the story may not be reliable, but the heart and soul of archaeology is the reconstruction of the past from its material remains. Thus, Schliemann and his early work at Troy deserve credit for drawing the world's attention to Troy as history instead of Troy as simply myth.

Although it has been much debated over the past few generations since he first excavated Troy, Heinrich Schliemann's role in changing the perception of Troy from just a story to a real place cannot be overestimated. Son of a disgraced clergyman, Schliemann made several fortunes around the world before turning his attention to Troy at the dawn of archaeology as a discipline. Shrewd businessman, manipulative showman, poor diplomat, liar, thief and pioneering archaeologist are just a few descriptions of him—probably all true—in circulation as early as 1875 while he was trying to change public opinion about Troy. Because his methods were suspect at best and downright destructive at worst, the debate is understandable. In retrospect, because he had hardly anyone to blaze a trail before him using proper archaeological methods as now practiced, time may be gentler on Schliemann in years to come, perhaps validating his pioneering stature while preserving some of his unsavory reputation.

These debates around Schliemann, centering on his apparent willingness to manipulate truth rather than on his meticulous field notes, often overlook that he attempted to differentiate layers of the Trojan past. Also too easily forgotten is his focus on ceramic artifacts, however fragmentary or mundane in appearance, because he hoped these might yield useful dating information. These are two of the backbones of modern archaeology. Stratigraphy (a term borrowed from geology) is concerned with the occupation layers of a site, and ceramic typology with analytical categories of ceramic vessels and their variations for dating and other purposes. Some of the earliest field techniques for these research methods were begun at Troy under Schliemann directly or under his well-chosen disciple, Wilhelm Dorpfeld (whom Schliemann knew to be careful and precise in the field, unlike himself), and later Dorpfeld's successor, Carl Blegen.

I was a graduate student at Athens in 1984 when I saw first-hand Schliemann's careful note-taking as an early archaeologist. I was duly impressed that Schliemann was perhaps the first archaeological investigator who not only carefully drew his own ceramic pots and wrote detailed descriptions of them—often in the exact context of where they were found and dated along with other data—but also did so in several languages in a fine careful script. Although I would not emulate his early methods or his character, that moment in 1984, when I could peer at his actual field notebooks, soon catapulted me lifelong into professional archaeology.

Matching Homer's epic poem to the landscape set precedents for other discoveries

Looking north from the top of the low scarred hill of Hisarlik above the plain in northern Turkey, the blue sea of the Dardanelles strait can rarely be seen, although seabirds still fly south over the trees here. The wind from the sea is often gusty, but the light summer breeze now is hardly enough to stir the blazing heat where cicadas drone incessantly, oblivious to the very different song recited by bards about this place for millennia. We now know this nondescript low hill above the plain was the site of fabled Troy, no longer just a myth but a historic place. Here is a small fraction of what Homer said about Troy in the *Iliad* (I.129–30; IV.30–34):

If ever Zeus gives into our hands the strong-walled citadel of Troy to
be plundered . . .
You are furious forever to bring down the strong-founded city of
Ilion? If you could walk through the gates and through the
towering ramparts . . .

Perhaps the most famous of all classical myths, Troy and the
Trojan War were immortalized by Homer in the dawn of Greek
literature. Actual Troy in the time of Homer (around 700 BC)
would hardly be memorable in 1850, as its location had been forgotten. One might see mostly overgrown ruins on the hill with
perhaps a few farmers' huts built into remnant walls sticking out
here and there above the olive trees that now dominated where
the watchtowers of the ancient fortress had jutted. But Troy in
song was already very recognizable, with gods and heroes inter-
locking in lives and loves that seemed larger than life. Remnants
of the older songs can still be found preserved in Homer, who is
himself a paradox and almost mythological. While he described a
place and landmarks that can still be matched, we really do not
know if a person named Homer actually existed or ever traveled
to Troy, although he was said to be from Ionia—which would be
western Turkey today, not far from Troy. Homer's epic poem is
all the more remarkable because he was also said to be blind. We
might conclude that for his epic *Iliad*, Homer used far older
sources with details he or someone else rewrote into marvelous
poetry, along with some of the most enduring mythology ever
imagined.

In Schliemann's time in the mid nineteenth century, the
prevailing opinion was that Troy was a fable. Frank Calvert was
there at Hisarlik before Schliemann by almost twenty years, since
1852. It is entirely probable that Calvert inspired Schliemann's
excavations, as many now maintain, and equally that it was his

idea that Hisarlik was Troy, not Schliemann's. While it is difficult to know whether it was Schliemann or his colleague Frank Calvert who, around 1872, first compared the local north-western Turkish landscape around Hisarlik to Homer's description, it was sufficiently important to establish that Mount Ida should be visible from the site of Troy, as Homer related through verse. Schliemann, either on his own or with Calvert's assistance, discovered firsthand that neither Bunarbashi at Bali Dagh Hill—the casual preference of a few historians who believed Homer could be accurate in landscape detail—or another site, at the village of Chiblak, clearly did not fit Homer in this respect. Other criteria where the topography was compared to the text included the plain where the Simois and Scamander rivers traversed, as well as visibility of the sea itself where ships would have been brought into harbor before later alluviation filled in much of the Bay of Besik. The hill of Hisarlik does fit these criteria, lying above the ancient watersheds of the Simois and Scamander streams and with Mount Ida just visible to the south, although the sea has greatly receded from full view. How much stock should be placed in poetry was a nagging question needing an answer, but the rediscovery of Troy provided a ready answer in the affirmative to all three landscape criteria. If Schliemann's source for matching the topography with the text was Frank Calvert and not from his own observations, Schliemann may have robbed Calvert of the ultimate glory of connecting Hisarlik to Troy and announcing Troy's rediscovery to the world. Ethical or not, Schliemann is rightly remembered as the larger-than-life controversial pioneer of archaeology far beyond Troy.

Both Schliemann and Calvert were anticipated, however, and possibly influenced by a Scottish geographer named Charles Maclaren in 1822, who maintained that "Issarlik" was the site of ancient Troy. Maclaren never visited the site for a firsthand confirmation as Calvert and Schliemann did, and his view was rejected by the scholarly community.

Following Schliemann's announcement to the world in 1872 that he had found Troy, partly by taking Homer's landscape account somewhat literally, a new tradition of matching ancient text to modern topography was greatly encouraged and it still persists to the present. Some more recent examples of archaeologists searching for ancient sites, cities and routes known from biblical texts include William Foxwell Albright, Yigael Yadin and Nelson Glueck, three of the most famous archaeologists of the twentieth century. Sites like Debir, Gibeon, Lachish and Masada in Israel were known from biblical texts and confirmed through cross-examining other ancient writings along with extensive site surveys, analyses and excavations. Even Sir Charles Leonard Woolley, who first excavated Ur in the 1920s, was inspired from the mention of the fabled biblical Ur. Other very recent examples in the Mediterranean world include looking for topographical matches of Hannibal's alpine route from classical texts like those of Polybius and Livy. Many historians and archaeologists, including myself, have done this for years, crossing the Alps on foot with the ancient texts in hand to compare the modern landscape with the classical authors' observations of the same landscape where possible.

Troy had many layers of civilization, stretching over thousands of years

We now know there were at least eight deep "layers" of culture at Troy, stretching back over four thousand years. Schliemann hopelessly muddled many of them and destroyed much of the evidence in his Great Trench, plowing right through the heart of the site to its earliest period and nearly to bedrock, but even Schliemann could establish some distinctions based on depth of burial and types of artifacts.

At the top of the hill, near the nineteenth-century surface, was the classical layer (stratum, in archaeological terms) now called Stratum IX, mostly from the Roman period around 85 BC to around AD 500. This city was named Ilium (or Novum Ilium), after its ancient name. The name Troy is also an ancient name, used in both the *Iliad* and the *Odyssey*. Yet long after its Bronze Age glory, perhaps Troy was not its most important classical name or the one by which the Greeks and others would have best known it. This Roman city had temples, theaters and other structures. Below this layer is Stratum VIII, dating from the Greek period, around 700 to 85 BC. (Apparently Alexander the Great visited Troy/Ilion around 332 BC.) This layer contains some older temples, theaters and buildings that were used as foundations for the newer ones.

Deeper yet, Stratum VII beneath it was much earlier, part of it dating to the Late Bronze Age from around 1250 to 1100 BC. There was no significant occupation between VII and VIII, as the site was mostly abandoned for around five hundred years from the Greek Dark Ages until the Greek colonial expansion in Ionia and much of western Anatolia. Stratum VII also corresponds to the last destruction of Troy before the recolonization, and some believe it best matches Homer's epic of a time at Troy that would lead to the conflicts between "Greeks" and "Trojans." Stratum VI beneath it is subdivided into different time periods, but most scholars believe it is the best fit for the Age of Heroes of the Mycenaean Era from around 1700 to 1250 BC, as described by Homer, most likely at the same time when a "Trojan War" could have taken place and when other Mycenaean cities were also suffering cataclysmic destruction. Stratum VI is also the period of maximum size for the Late Bronze Age, the time when the great walls were built. A later culture of early Greeks called these walls "Cyclopean masonry" because the individual stones were massive and thought too large for humans to quarry and carry, which suggests technology had fallen into a doldrum by their time. Strata III through V beneath Stratum VI have waxing and waning periods of growth between around 2200 and 1700 BC.

Nearly at the deepest level of this long-occupied place, Stratum II beneath all these prior layers is dated from around 2400 BC to the end of the Early Bronze Age around 2200 BC. This is a much smaller town and is the purported period from which Schliemann dug his famous "Priam's Treasure," despite the fact that it is about a thousand years older than he thought. Stratum I goes back to the beginning of the Early Bronze Age around 3000 until around 2400 BC, and likely before 3000 BC into Neolithic times when the fortress was hardly more than a hilltop, perhaps surrounded with a wooden palisade around it close to the natural bedrock.

Although Schliemann gravely misinterpreted the data for understanding the many different cultural layers at Troy, there were no archaeological precedents for him to follow in Anatolia. His followers and successors, including Wilhelm Dorpfeld from 1890 onward, Carl Blegen in the 1930s, and Manfred Korfmann and others in the 1980s and 1990s, have calibrated and refined the study of Troy's many layers, probing deeper than sixty feet. In this way, we can marvel at its long history, not continuously occupied but rebuilt many times because of its strategic placement on one of the most important trade routes between Europe and Asia, along the vital waterway that connected the Black Sea to the Mediterranean along the Dardanelles strait.

Schliemann, whatever his motives and methods, persuaded the world Troy had existed

In his multiple field campaigns at Troy, from 1870 through 1890, Schliemann did what no one else had done: he connected literature and landscape where no contemporary tradition existed, and then he eventually persuaded the scholarly world of his discovery.

The controversial Schliemann was attacked for his 1872 identification of Hisarlik with Troy—mostly because he challenged the prevailing opinion, circulating as scholarship—and justifiably for naming something he found and smuggled from Hisarlik in 1873 "Priam's Treasure" without any proof of a connection to Priam from inscriptions. He drew the attention of the world to both Troy as a possible real place and to Homer as a recorder of such likely events as an earlier Trojan War in the *Iliad*. When his book *Troy and Its Remains* came out in London in 1874, his many critics accused him of everything from hyperactive imagination to adultery, theft and financial charlatanry. Many critics stooped to absurd comments such as: "If Troy never existed, how could he have found it?"

But Schliemann also had his defenders who agreed with him. While they did not necessarily admire him, they at least grudgingly rallied to his identification of Hisarlik with Troy. Some were notable scholars of the day, even if in a minority now proven right. These academic "allies" ultimately included Dr. Rudolf Virchow of Berlin; Charles Newton of the British Museum in London; another early archaeologist, the Orientalist and linguist Professor Friedrich Max Müller of Oxford—with whom Schliemann exchanged at least seventy letters—and Professor

Archibald Henry Sayce, another Orientalist and Mesopotamian authority also at Oxford, among others.

Even Schliemann's greatest modern detractor, David Traill, who has painstakingly "excavated" Schliemann's life and problematic dealings, acknowledges that Schliemann's notebooks are mostly "truthful and accurate" records of his Hisârlik finds. While laying bare the deceits of Schliemann, Traill concedes that "The excavations . . . of Schliemann rank among the most important in the history of archaeology."

The Trojan War—if historical—was not because of a woman but over trade rights

Myth tells us one story, history another. We read from the myths and legends of the Greeks and Romans that the abduction of Helen by the Trojan prince Paris was the cause of the Trojan War. According to these legends, Troy's destruction was brought about when Paris chose Aphrodite (Venus in the Roman myth) over Hera (Juno) and Athena (Minerva) in the famous beauty contest between the goddesses.

As different mythologers variously narrate, Zeus (Jupiter) had invited all the gods to a wedding between Peleus and Thetis because Thetis, a goddess, was pregnant with Zeus's son. According to prophecies of the Delphic Oracle, this son would become greater than his father. Zeus couldn't allow a son greater than himself, so he made sure she would marry a weak mortal king, Peleus, to get around the prophecy. It was a rigged contest because he gave the Apple of Discord (inscribed "to the fairest") to Aphrodite rather than to either of them. Young Paris was riddled with arrows of desire by Eros (Cupid) and was not interested in a harmonious marriage blessed by Hera or conquering and ruling the world with Athena's wisdom, whereas Aphrodite promised Paris the most beautiful woman in the world. The myth has Paris choosing Aphrodite and thus earning the undying hatred of Hera and Athena.

Aphrodite made good on her promise when Paris arrived in Sparta. Helen, wife of King Menelaus of Sparta, eloped with Paris and they both fled to Troy. The Greeks needed vengeance on Troy to defend her and to restore their national pride. This myth version of the cause of the Trojan War is a wonderful story but is unlikely and lacks any historical basis.

The famous William Gladstone, prime minister of Britain, was somewhat of a scholar, writing *Homer and the Homeric Age* between 1858 and 1876. There he suggested the Trojan War was actually a civil war. Either he was influenced and encouraged by Schliemann or Schliemann was influenced by Gladstone, as both cultivated each other's opinions when Gladstone was prime minister in several different British governments.

In reality, history suggests a different story from the Homeric myth. All one has to do is look at a map to see that Troy is situated in northwestern Anatolia—Turkey today. This location is the bridge where Europe and Asia meet along the Dardanelles, the watery strait between the Black Sea and the eastern Mediterranean, especially the Aegean Sea.

Troy lay directly on the trade route between the East and West, and the currents and winds converged in such a way as to bring water traffic into Troy's harbor on the Bay of Besik whether the ships sought it or not. Troy either taxed the stalled merchandise or became an arbiter of trade. Both the people who traded in the East along the Black Sea and beyond and those in the West who sought Eastern luxuries could not avoid Troy, and they had to pay more in duty or tax to these Trojan middlemen who controlled the strait.

Due to its unique strategic geographic position, Troy could act as a trade nexus, where goods from both directions would collect thanks to the wind and water currents. This is how Troy became an emporium for the meeting of West and East.

So if there was a Trojan War, it was most likely a trade war where others tried to conquer Troy in order to break its monopoly, in an attempt to reduce tariffs on whatever trade came through and eliminate the higher price tag added on by the Trojans. The warlike Mycenaean Greeks of the thirteenth century BC, then called the Achaeans, were more likely to confront Troy than their neighbors. The Hittites to the southeast of Troy in central Anatolia were also at some economic risk over the Trojan trade monopoly to the west, but no epic poem has survived narrating their struggles with the issue that the Greeks recorded, however poetically, in the *Iliad*. Thus the Trojan War—or many such battles combined in legend—was essentially a turf war.

What kind of trade goods would have come through Troy from east to west and vice versa? Luxury goods bound for the West would take this northern route when the Mesopotamian route to the south was wracked by instability or brigand tribes or lawless robbers. This is most likely when there was no centralized government with an army large enough to protect trade. History tells us there was just this sort of power vacuum in Mesopotamia in the Late Bronze Age between the fifteenth and twelfth centuries BC, making Troy's route more likely since merchants and traders almost always sought the cheapest route for moving goods.

Textiles—possibly even silk—came to the West along this northern route, skirting the Caucasus Mountains and the Caspian Sea to the east. Gems and precious stones like blue lapis lazuli could follow the same route. Spices and salt for food and perfumes might also come this way if the southern route was too dangerous, as mentioned. The ancestors of the early Greeks would have wanted to trade their wine, olive oil, and maybe their grain or even their gold, silver, copper or other metals for eastern luxury goods they could not produce for themselves. But Troy offered an ideal emporium due to its seaway location between the Black Sea and the Aegean Sea. War over this trade would have been inevitable and so some kind of Trojan war is more likely historical than the myths suggest. Naturally, a myth narrative has more human interest when it is a fight over a beautiful woman than over bolts of cloth.

The Trojan Horse is not just myth— horses first arrived here from the East

As mentioned, mythology can sometimes contain a kernel of historical truth. The presence of a giant wooden horse in the story of Troy symbolizes far more than hidden danger. Everyone knows the symbol of the Trojan Horse, but what is really behind the myth of this horse and why does this animal so symbolize Troy's downfall? Troy was famous for its horse breeding even in myth. In Greek myth, the sea god Poseidon was also the god of horses and one of the gods, along with Apollo, who helped build the walls of Troy. The crown prince of Troy was Hector, whom the last line of the *Iliad* described as "Hector, tamer of horses." The long plume on Hector's great helmet was also of horsehair and many other quotations in the *Iliad* link Hector and the Trojans with horses. Thus the myth idea of a Trojan Horse as a trap sprung by Odysseus for the people of Troy was not as far-fetched as it might seem, since this was already an attractive image to them and one with which they readily identified.

Historians of animal breeding tell us that around 2000 BC, horses first found their way into the Mediterranean world,

funneled from central Asia through the Black Sea and the
Dardanelles strait, most likely also through Troy, as this was
clearly the connecting point between Asia and Europe, established in trade. They were ridden by migrating peoples and were
traded and bred as beasts of burden and as steeds for war chariots,
the juggernaut of war in the ancient world that would give powerful advantage to whoever had horses over those who did not. A
horse in this myth story can thus be a clue to the history behind
Troy, an image of migrating peoples who rode this animal as they
moved over the steppes and ultimately through the same gateway
of Troy as exotic trade goods—perhaps even first seen as centaurs
by the westerners who would not have recognized the duo of man
and domesticated animal. This mythic horse motif is yet another
possible piece in the jigsaw puzzle found behind the rediscovery
of Troy, suggesting other fascinating answers waiting to be found
when the significance of Troy is further understood, uncovering
more historical facts embedded under the layers of myth.

Texts from the Bronze Age Hittites show they knew Ilion as Wilusa, proving Troy's existence at that time

Language and linguistics continue to add more concrete evidence to Troy's existence as the widening ripples of knowledge
from its rediscovery settle other old debates. Facts of archaeology
are thus connected to linguistic discoveries. Specialists in ancient
Hittite culture (1500–1100 BC) in Anatolia—modern Turkey—
have found Troy in that ancient language as well. Hans Güter-
bock, for example, has shown that the name Ilion in Greek is
closely related to the Hittite name for a place that must have been
Troy. The apparent Hittite place-name for Troy was Wilusa, and

this word also parallels Mycenaean Proto-Greek words that survived in Linear B texts. In the most ancient Greek, a "w" sound
often precedes words beginning in vowels. So tracing the Hittite
word and following early Greek, if we drop the "w" from *Wilusa*,
it becomes *Ilusa*, which is recognizably similar to *Ilion*.

Furthermore, the Hittite name for the marauding and seafaring people who colonized or traded with their western coast-
lands and islands—the Aegean shore of modern Turkey—was
Ahhiyawa. This is again recognizable as the same name by which
the Mycenaean Greeks are called in Homer, the people from
Achaea, whose name survives throughout classical history as the
Achaeans. Although a myth poem, why shouldn't Homer's *Iliad*
agree with linguists that both myth and fragments of ancient language in some way record the fact that a number of Greeks and
Trojans could identify each other by name? Like the archaeological data coming from excavations at Troy, showing hybridized
culture from both East and West, ancient language uncovered
because of Troy's rediscovery now makes more sense. In fact,
this new linguistic evidence for Ilion/Troy as Wilusa and the
Achaeans themselves would most likely not have been linked
had the site and its importance not been rediscovered.

These and similar linguistic evidences flesh out how Troy was
not just the subject of an epic poem of Homeric lore but increasingly shown to be a historical place, as pioneering archaeology in
the last half of the nineteenth century proved.

Modern excavations at Troy continue to show its importance

J. Lawrence Angel was a famous paleoanthropologist from
the Smithsonian who paved the way for archaeosteology, the

study of ancient human bones. He proved some years ago that cemeteries around Troy yielded an important fact. From the burials in the area Dr. Angel deduced that there were three kinds of skull shapes in the region: an Aegean one, which would be European or probably Greek or Hellenic from the west; an Anatolian one, which could be identified with the Hittites from the east and southeast; and a third that was hybridized between the two, especially found around the region of Troy. The suggestion is that because it was an emporium for trade, Troy had a mixed population of Hittite and Mycenaean ethnic elements where such physical characteristics would be blended over time.

Starting in 1988, Manfred Korfmann from the University of Tübingen began directing a new archaeology project at Troy. Collaborating with colleagues from all over the world, including Machteld Mellink from Bryn Mawr College and Brian Rose from the University of Cincinnati, Korfmann's bold conclusions are not accepted by all, but the drama he has unfolded again drew attention to Troy. Korfmann died in 2005, as did Mellink in 2006, but their monumental work has underscored Troy's historical importance since the late nineteenth and early twentieth centuries, especially in light of a new research question: did the Trojan War really happen?

Korfmann's staff innovated such current remote sensing techniques as GPR (ground-penetrating radar) and magnetometry and discovered new material evidence that is still debated but extremely valuable to archaeology. Many critics had earlier doubted the ruins at Hisarlik as the location of Troy because its enclosing walls were too small to surround a city of epic proportions. The new scientific research discovered portions of datable Late Bronze Age walls down on the plain, far from the citadel higher on the hill. Thus, the hill of Hisarlik is most likely only the acropolis, in keeping with ancient cities, and the city of Troy was much larger than previously thought. Aerial photography even shows the likely "footprint" of the old city now outlined in olive groves where modern agricultural production cannot be so easily cultivated because of irregular ground, possibly hiding the rest of the city of Troy. Korfmann's modern findings actually also proved one of Schliemann's (or Calvert's) early intuitions true, that the citadel was only a small part of old Troy, as Schliemann wrote in *Ilios* in 1873:

> Up to the beginning I had believed that the hill of Hissarlik, where I was excavating, marked the site of the Trojan citadel only; and it is the fact that Hissarlik was the acropolis of Novum Ilium . . .

By Novum Ilium, Schliemann meant the much later Roman city that was also located there. Schliemann went on to claim, however, that his excavation results contradicted this intuition. This hunch could have led to a scientifically valid deduction had he dug in the right places, as Korfmann appears to have done over a century later.

Perhaps the most exciting element of the most recent archaeological research at Troy is that Korfmann's teams have also found substantial evidence of warfare, excavating buried arrowheads, sometimes even embedded in the burned material archaeologists call carbonized "ash lenses" from burning wood. While the evidence is still being sorted and analyzed, Korfmann's legacy may well be ultimately seen as proof of at least one Trojan war, even if only on a regional scale and not, as epic Homeric literature related, in such widespread magnificent terms as have inspired artists, poets and historians alike ever since.

Conclusion

The discipline of archaeology as material history began with Troy's excavation, changing once and for all the misperception that our only sources for understanding ancient history were in written texts. The soil and what lies in it can also be read by a different kind of historian: the archaeologist. However Troy's history and its sometimes questionable pioneering excavators like Schliemann will be revised, edited and corrected, Troy's reemergence from its buried past in 1871–72 remains a seminal discovery that shook the world and rewrote history.

Chapter 3

Nineveh's Assyrian Library
The Key to Mesopotamia

Kuyunjik mound, outside Mosul, 1849

Alone for the first time in weeks, he had waited at least a decade for this moment, crossing continents and braving long miles over stormy seas and hot deserts, listening to the clamor and din of calls to prayer, breathing exotic spices in tented markets, and haggling with caravans of camel drivers in a babble of languages. It was all behind him now and the moon was rising as he climbed the huge mound, his long shadow breaking the silvery light. His name was Austen Henry Layard, and he had been searching several years for the famous lost city of Nineveh. Although he had trained as a lawyer back in London, so far away now, and was serving as a young diplomat, it was antiquity that really drove him, ancient history that excited him most. One of his favorite reads was the old biblical prophetic book of Nahum, whose poetry described the fall of Nineveh. His love of the mostly forgotten ancient world was why, two years before, he had assembled a team of Ottoman workers and obtained a *firman*, a permit to dig the mound of Nimrud some miles away. His valuable experience at Nimrud led him to the nearby city of Mosul, where a few junk sellers in the marketplace had showed him a few dusty objects. When he asked the source, they had pointed to this mound of Kuyunjik he was now ascending.

As he looked over this huge hill that stretched away for at least an acre in every direction, Layard suspected the dried mud lumps of rubble and deep furrows of earth showing in moonlit relief were all that was left of old broken walls. This had once been a fortress, and judging by its size, a mighty one. One particular rampart, mostly shapeless, even seemed like it could have been a gateway in its deeper shadows. He strode over to it, noting it must shelter lizards in the daylight. He decided he would start right here in the morning, as soon as the workers arrived for whom he had bargained with their clan chief. It was now time to return to the sleepy town of Mosul, and Layard knew he would dream that night the same dream about Nineveh. He hoped with all his passion for history that this hill was really it. Descending, he heard the cries of jackals in the distance and an owl flew across the moon looking for a mouse or two before dawn, a day that would not come soon enough for Austen Henry Layard.... However much this version of the story may differ from other accounts, Layard knew he was hot on the trail of the ancient city.

Layard indeed found Nineveh in those next few days in 1849, his workers digging out the massive palace gates with their bearded demigods, gigantic beast bodies and great eagle wings. Although it wasn't confirmed as Nineveh for at least a decade or so by the clay text tablets, written in cuneiform, found in an archive dug up from one of the former palaces on this hill that nature had started and humans had finished, Layard's dream was fulfilled. The archive was what remained of the Royal Assyrian

Library. What we know now from this royal library, created by King Ashurbanipal, has vastly changed history. Through Layard's discovery, we came to understand a Nineveh that was both similar and dissimilar to the legendary biblical city, and that surprisingly, the Hanging Gardens of Babylon may actually be in Nineveh rather than Babylon. Unearthing the Royal Assyrian Library revealed a whole history previously lost—containing a huge body of Mesopotamian lore, science, medicine, magic, and epic poetry and literature like the Epic of Gilgamesh. When Layard published his seminal exploration book, *Nineveh and Its Remains*, it was to a public with a huge new appetite for history. A few years later, George Smith's discovery of the Flood Tablet became pivotal for biblical studies as these connect to the other ancient Near Eastern traditions, many far older.

This riveting find of the Assyrian king Ashurbanipal's royal library in Nineveh brought to light a whole library of cuneiform texts, not only from ancient Assyria but also texts copied from far older Sumerian, Akkadian, Babylonian and other great civilizations. For the most part this great literature was now seen for the first time in the West. This discovery changed world literature, as demonstrated in such works as the Epic of Gilgamesh, Enuma Elish and the Law Code of Hammurabi, among so many other texts. From 1847 onward, Nineveh was no longer a fable, but a reality.

Assyrian background

In 612 BC Nineveh, one of the world's greatest cities, was utterly destroyed. Nineveh had been the lofty capital of the Assyrians, whose conquests had made their name feared throughout the lands of the ancient Near East, from the deserts of Egypt to the mountains of Persia. Assyria had been the world's first military empire, a juggernaut that had laid waste to city after city, besieging them with massive armies. Its commanding rulers had styled themselves as kings of all kings. Assyrian cruelty was legendary; captives were skewered on poles or decapitated, their children were blinded and their royal families were dragged off into captivity, yanked on chains connected to bronze hooks pierced through their tongues. If the Assyrians did not invent psychological warfare, they certainly practiced it well. In their seemingly invincible prime between the ninth and seventh centuries BC, their clever propaganda about what they would do to any resisting peoples often made their trembling enemies capitulate as soon as they heard the clank of Assyrian armor approaching.

But now it was the Assyrians' turn in the balance scale of history. Weakened by years of neglecting internal matters, with an economy dependent on slavery and war booty rather than trade, there was hardly any unconquered wealth left to seize. The southern vassal state of Babylon had risen up under its dynamic and charismatic ruler, Nabopolassar, father of the more famous Nebuchadnezzar who sacked Jerusalem. Nabopolassar persuaded his people that the Assyrians were now only a shadow of their former mighty selves. Although it had been attacked a few years before by the Medes to the east, Nineveh had survived, but now the city was ripe for the plucking. Nabopolassar quickly marched an army up the Tigris and launched an attack that soon had the Assyrians trapped in their royal city by a prolonged siege that gave the residents no respite. Nabopolassar could count on the fact that no one would come to the rescue of the hated Assyrians. In the aftermath, the Babylonians would destroy almost everything, yet preserve something marvelous: the thousands of clay tablets in the royal library.

Nineveh's towering thirty-foot crenellated walls were punctuated by city gates of thick bronze-sheathed wood now resounding with the heavy blows of battering rams. Under cover of huge

shields where the defenders' arrows failed to reach, the Babylonians' fierce assault was deadly. The imposing gates of Nineveh
were breached at last and the remaining defending soldiers were
overwhelmed by wave after wave of Babylonians and their allies,
all desperately ready to throw off the Assyrian yoke. Even in
faraway Israel, the voice of Nahum the prophet would be heard in
song, "Nineveh is fallen, the city of blood where ever is heard the
sound of chains." Nobody outside Assyria wept.

The years of pent-up vengeance and resentment against
Nineveh gave its destroyers added incentive as flames devoured
the great roof beams of cedar. Some of the sun-dried mud bricks
and myriad other clay objects were fired as if the entire city were
a giant kiln. Whatever was left of the great city built of mud
brick turned to dust over the ensuing years. Several thousand
years later as the Ottoman empire extended over the land
between the Tigris and Euphrates, Europeans no longer traveled
there often, and the Assyrians became no more than a dim name
in history. Later, Nineveh would be so thoroughly forgotten that
the only memory of it was found in the Bible. Skeptics like
Voltaire in the French Enlightenment of the eighteenth century
found this biblical citation of Assyria to be a dubious proof of
existence and called Nineveh a myth much like the rest of sacred
scripture.

But not everybody thought of Nineveh in those terms. England was filled with churchmen who took the English Bible seriously. The vicars of the Church of England who accompanied
the growing British empire into foreign lands were passionate
about connecting history and the Bible to their travels in the
exotic ruins of the Holy Land and the ancient Near East. Although it was not yet called archaeology as we would later know
it, antiquities and ruins were the educated hobby of British
churchmen and many of their parishioners. A people brought up

on history and the Bible would devour journals, diaries and travelogues that would satisfy an appetite for connecting names and places from Sunday school.

It was the French who first tried to find Nineveh, by sending Paul Emile Botta as their consul to Mosul. Botta found the palace of Khorsabad but not Nineveh. Because consulates were desirable posts for collectors and passionate amateur historians, an enterprising young British citizen promptly garnered a British diplomatic post in Constantinople (Istanbul). He managed to persuade the British ambassador to the Ottoman sultan there to help underwrite excavations in Mesopotamia. The young British lawyer was Austen Henry Layard (1817–94), whom we have already met, and in the year 1845 he discovered the ancient Assyrian site of Nimrud, although he mistakenly called it Nineveh. His next expedition took him to Kuyunjik mound just outside Mosul, which became his greatest archaeological success.

In 1849–50, after Austen Henry Layard discovered Nineveh and the palaces of Sennacherib and Ashurbanipal on Kuyunjik mound, the royal acropolis of the Assyrians, Mesopotamia's layered history began gradually to be understood. It is unclear who first unearthed the royal library of Assyria in King Ashurbanipal's palace—Layard or his assistant Hormuzd Rassam—but the archive room containing tens of thousands of clay tablets was preserved when Nineveh fell in 612 BC. Layard excavated the library archive, which must stand as one of the greatest treasures in world history, not the least because the recorded tablets opened up a whole ancient world previously unknown. This treasure is all the more unique in that it is not gold, silver and gems, but mere clay, and its value is in the words recorded on the tablets. So many years after the fires of 612 BC, Layard apparently knew the words of Nahum by heart, and the new clay Nineveh texts his discovery would eventually unearth would become more valuable than anything else he undertook.

Nineveh was both similar and dissimilar to the legendary biblical city

This wasn't the same near fictive biblical city where the prophet Jonah came reluctantly with a message of repentance, an imaginary place where multiple chariots could race abreast on the broad walls, a city so large that it would take a man three days to cross it, according to the book of Jonah. Nineveh's wall, almost fourteen miles long, enclosed more than 1,800 acres and a population that must have been well over one hundred thousand, which made it the largest city of the world at the time, larger even than Babylon. About the only part of the city that was fully stone was this enclosing wall. Many of its fifteen great gates were named after Assyrian gods—the Ashur Gate (the chief god of Assyria), the Adad Gate (the storm god), the Sin Gate (the moon god), the Shamash Gate (the sun god) and others.

David Stronach's most recent excavations in 1989–90 uncovered quite a few skeletons surrounded by their weapons and some even skewered with arrowheads. These were a few of the Assyrian defenders who died in 612 BC in the burned rubble of the Halzi Gate.

After the tablets, perhaps the most important archaeological artifacts are the incredible reliefs unearthed, depicting scenes such as the famous siege and destruction of the Judean city of Lachish by Sennacherib around 702 BC and the Lion Hunt reliefs of Ashurbanipal. These reliefs have been called the most important masterpieces of Assyrian art. Sennacherib, the Assyrian king who sacked Judah, had an intimidating palace that was over 630 feet by 600 feet ("the palace without rival"). The walls of its nearly eighty rooms were decorated with reliefs in which vassal kings in servitude were forced to look and tremble at Assyrian military efficiency and with scene after scene of Assyrian battle prowess. Such reliefs covered several linear miles of walls.

The tablets, however, are priceless for other reasons: they tell us in amazing detail about ancient Mesopotamia—information that we would otherwise not know. We call these tablets cuneiform because of the way they are written. *Cuneus* in Latin means "wedge" and on these tablets a small wooden stylus was pressed into the soft clay to make an impression that looks like a wedge-shaped dent. The clay tablets were then left to harden in the hot Near Eastern sun to dry them out and make them somewhat permanent as long as they are kept out of water. If they are heated high enough by being close to or in a fire, they become almost like stone and truly permanent.

On the smaller mound at Nineveh, a tomb shrine to Jonah can still be found, perhaps to commemorate this same biblical prophet in Islamic legend. The shrine's Arabic name is Nebi Yunas, which means "Prophet Jonah." The people of Mosul had a legend that the larger mound of Kuyunjik to the northwest was jestingly said to be the burial site of the whale that swallowed Jonah.

When choosing the site for his city, King Sennacherib (ruling from 705 to circa 681 BC) knew the location of Nineveh was vital because it lay at the junction of two rivers. His city would also reuse the hill location of a much older site. The Tigris River flowed south along Nineveh's city wall and the Khosr River joined from the northeast. Son of King Sargon, Sennacherib refounded the old city around 700 BC and moated the area around it for defense, also bringing in water via aqueducts. The imported water, from over eighteen separate aqueducts, was partly for his people but also for his famous gardens, some of whose trees and plants can be seen fed by these aqueducts in a palace relief.

We now know that King Ashurbanipal was motivated as much for personal reasons to create this great archive of Mesopotamian lore as for altruism. The king wanted to learn how to read, which naturally satisfied his immense curiosity, but also because he mistrusted his augurs, priests and scribes. Superstitious like all his royal predecessors, the king wanted to be free from manipulation from his clergy, who wielded immense power and could easily control a weaker-minded king. Ashurbanipal would be able to keep his handlers in check by verifying what they claimed to be reading from ancient texts in order to influence imperial policy. Assyrians loved to corroborate and emphasize their strengths by examples from their history, and this included the legacies of previous dynasties and even allies or subjugated enemies.

The immediate outcome was that Ashurbanipal thus collected the greatest assemblage of ancient texts from all over Mesopotamia, employing hundreds of scribes to copy material sent by his command from places like Elam, old Akkad and even older Sumer, Babylon and Susa, especially older texts in temples throughout the Assyrian empire. Part of the king's policy was to keep the original tablets, or whatever form they took; he'd have them copied at least once, then send copies back to the sources rather than the original primary text. This means that instead of storing only Assyrian texts from the seventh century, roughly around 645 BC, his library also stored—and we also now have—texts going back two and a half millennia before Ashurbanipal, in their original state and often with a copy to boot. Apparently these archives in Ashurbanipal's palace were organized thematically, and there were also key tablets that served as filing systems for referencing all the tablets. Although not all have survived, the quantity and variety of texts from Nineveh are truly staggering.

Unearthing the Royal Assyrian Library revealed a whole history previously lost

There is some debate as to the exact timing of the discovery of the archive during the excavations of Ashurbanipal's palace on the north portion of the Kuyunjik mound. Considerable argument continues about whether it was Austen Henry Layard or his assistant Hormuzd Rassam who found the primary archive of more than twenty-six thousand fragmentary tablets (today mostly housed in the British Museum). The total number of complete Nineveh tablets was most likely around ten thousand before Nineveh's destruction. It is not debated that Layard excavated at Nineveh in 1849 before permanently leaving archaeology sometime in 1851 or 1852 for a career in Parliament. Some archaeological records state that Layard found the bulk of his tablets in Sennacherib's palace but merely had them shipped from Mosul to London's British Museum in baskets because he could not read cuneiform. Layard is not to be blamed for this ignorance since hardly anyone in 1850 could translate anything in cuneiform but the most cursory material. Georg Grotefend's contributions from 1803 and Henry Rawlinson's in 1837, both working from a trilingual inscription made in a cliff wall at Bisistun (then called Behistun), were still very much a collective work in progress. Hormuzd Rassam, who followed Layard, continued to excavate Ashurbanipal's palace for the British and also found an archive of tablets around 1852 but neither Layard's nor

Rassam's records have made it easy to reconcile or separate Nineveh's archives.

Therefore it is most likely that two separate archives have been merged—without adequate excavation documentation—under the rubric of Ashurbanipal's library. On the other hand, we have good authority for the literate Ashurbanipal commissioning his own palace archive, and so he should receive most of the credit for the library.

The material from Nineveh's archives has essentially given birth to a plethora of new disciplines that would hardly have existed to their full extent without these texts, the key to opening up lost ancient Near Eastern languages. The Assyrians preserved not only their own culture but that of their ancestors and contemporary and ancient neighbors, even those whose texts had to be translated into Assyrian. Some of these new fields include not only Assyriology but Sumerology, Akkadian studies and many more.

Layard's exploration book, Nineveh and Its Remains, *fed popular enthusiasm*

Back in London after 1849, Austen Henry Layard oversaw the publication of several exploration books from his Near Eastern sojourn, including *Nineveh and Its Remains* around 1850. The book became an overnight bestseller, in part because it proved the existence of this biblical city to English readers of the Bible. Layard wrote well, and his books read almost like travelogues. Here he colorfully relates excavating a giant winged bull from Khorsabad:

> It was a moment of great anxiety. The drums and shrill pipes of the Kurdish musicians increased the din and confusion caused

by the war-cry of the Arabs, who were half frantic with excitement . . . Away went the bull . . . The cables and ropes stretched
more and more. Dry from the climate, as they felt the strain,
they creaked and threw out dust. Water was thrown over them,
but in vain, for they all broke together when the sculpture was
within four or five feet of the rollers. The bull was precipitated
to the ground. Those who held the ropes, thus suddenly released, followed its example and were rolling, one over the
other, in the dust. A sudden silence succeeded to the clamor. I
rushed into the trenches, prepared to find the bull in many
pieces. It would be difficult to describe my satisfaction, when I
saw it lying precisely where I wished to place it, and uninjured!

Layard's popular accounts were in many ways better than his
archaeological records, but this was in the days before the exact-
ing artifact documentation and finds processing of a modern
scientific expedition. Yet his devoted readers in London soon ate
up every word, especially a young boy named George Smith a
few years later around 1856 or so.

George Smith's discovery of the Flood Tablet became a pivot for biblical studies

Perhaps the most exciting discovery in Mesopotamian texts is
the "moment" when George Smith (1840–76) found the Flood
Tablet in the British Museum cuneiform collection from Nineveh
and translated it in 1872. The son of a laborer, George Smith did
not receive a high level of education. He was apprenticed at age
fourteen as an engraver of banknotes—where he honed his keen
powers of observation—and soon turned to archaeology after

reading Layard's accounts of Nineveh. Smith was so intensely interested in cuneiform that like a sponge he absorbed every possible source, hanging out at the British Museum until he eventually attracted the attention of Sir Henry Rawlinson, the "Father of Assyriology," who was one of the major decipherers of cuneiform, especially the Behistun Stone. Rawlinson had Smith appointed as an assistant in the Near Eastern Department at the British Museum and Smith, with his keen eyesight and agile mind, learned to read laborious Assyrian cuneiform when this discipline was still in its infancy.

Like one in love, the passionate Smith was always trying to piece together the many thousand fragmentary tablets, some burned in the fire of Nineveh's destruction, some even melted, and many others in an excellent baked state from the fire of 612 BC, which actually preserved them by altering their sun-dried clay (which rain could dissolve over time) to fired ceramic. The fire in Nineveh was one of the luckier circumstances in archaeology, because a fire usually leads to ruin and loss; instead all these valuable artifacts were preserved. As he rummaged through museum boxes and baskets, some of them newly numbered and cataloged, others in their original packing from Layard or Rassam, Smith's eye was caught by one fine tablet. The record for this particular piece said it had been excavated by Layard, and its accession and collection number was ANE K 3375—the K and the low number showing that it was an early Kuyunjik tablet. Smith blew dust off of it and bent down to read its very fine text as he ran his finger along the spidery cuneiform only a few tenths of an inch high.

Smith was immediately astonished. He quickly read it again to check himself, not believing what he read. It was an unknown account from the Epic of Gilgamesh in Assyrian that told of Utnapishtim, who built a boat at the gods' urgent command and filled it with all life. When the rains came, the earth was flooded for six days and all humanity was destroyed except for Utnapish-tim and those on his boat. Landing on a mountaintop called Nimush, Utnapishtim released a dove, then a swallow, but they came back. Utnapishtim then released a raven, which never returned, so he knew it had found dry land. Smith, like nearly everyone of the Victorian era, knew the Bible's account of Noah and the flood, in Genesis 6–11, practically by heart. But for the first time here was another version that seemed not to come from the Bible! Smith was so agitated that he ran around the room, jumping up and down and even unbuttoning his clothes.

Smith soon presented his discovery before the Society of Bib-lical Archaeology in London and then to the stunned world. Sadly George Smith died young, only a few years later, while in the Near East searching for further archaeological caches of texts. No one has ever found anything as greatly revealing about a whole portion of the ancient world as the Royal Assyrian Library, but there may yet be an archive still buried that will be found and made known.

Besides its deserved status as the most famous of the entire cuneiform collection of the British Museum, why else is this tablet in Room 55, Case 10 so significant? Part of the answer lies in the obvious: it confirmed the Bible with an external unrelated artifact far from ancient Israel. But another part of the answer is that this ordinary-looking tablet also raised enormous questions about the priority of texts. Which came first and which borrowed from the other? Now we know not only that hundreds of texts from Mesopotamia parallel the familiar biblical stories that fit the Bronze Age like a hand in a glove, but that there are thousands of texts much older than the Bible. These include Sumerian accounts from 2500 BC and earlier, texts like the famous Law Code of Hammurabi and others that are later echoed in the Law of Moses. One conclusion must be that the Bible is not the only repository of ancient law and literature and it is also very much influenced by the older texts. This theory was more revolutionary in 1872 than now, and it created intellectual conflicts for many religionists in the late nineteenth century at a time when new discoveries in every field were challenging long-held beliefs and dogmas. This one small cuneiform tablet preserved from the destruction of Nineveh over 2,600 years ago, only about seven inches long and six inches wide and one inch thick, led the way to whole new textual revelations that changed the way ancient history was being taught and learned all over the world.

The library contains a huge body of Mesopotamian literature, science and medicine

The Nineveh library is now our primary textual source for understanding ancient Mesopotamian life from thousands of years ago in the Sumerian, Akkadian, and Babylonian cultures of the Bronze Age. These texts have recorded thousands of events in Mesopotamian history as well as revealed Babylonian astronomy and Mesopotamian science, medicine, geography, botany, philosophy, religion, cosmology, magic and many other fields. Ancient Mesopotamian history is no longer a closed book for us but a vibrant animated world of people so very much like us, with common fears, hopes and life experiences.

Because we have over ten thousand tablets broken into twenty-six thousand fragments, we can now better understand ancient economies of Mesopotamia through their tax records, animal and farm inventories, legal cases, inheritance codes, recipes, medical cases, magic spells, garden lore, student copybooks and even how teachers disciplined schoolchildren. Indeed a whole world that was previously lost has been found and with it our common human history. This library soon became the proving place for reading cuneiform texts from the Ubaid culture long before Sumer (almost 6,000 years ago) to Achaeminid Persia (2,500 years ago), since they all used symbols from a long pictorial evolution that eventually became cuneiform. The library of Nineveh, preserved by the caprice of selective destruction, opened a door that is widening still with each new text translation out of the thousands of tablets.

The Hanging Gardens of Babylon may actually be in Nineveh

The original Seven Wonders of the Ancient World were recorded by various writers in antiquity, from Herodotus, a Greek historian (although he did not compile a list of countable wonders), to Diodorus Siculus, a Roman historian, among others. One of these original seven wonders, called the Hanging Gardens of Babylon, was said to have been built by Nebuchadnezzar around 600 BC.

But the original "hanging gardens" may not have been Babylonian or even in Babylon. Because we can now read the scribes' texts, commanded to be written by Ashurbanipal and his grandfather Sennacherib, we know they also had gardens in Nineveh that "hung" or were terraced. These gardens were filled with thousands of imported plants and trees, brought from all over the known world, including cedars from Lebanon and pines from Aleppo. We also know Sennacherib's canals and aqueducts were not just for his people in Nineveh but for watering his pleasure gardens. We know from the Assyrian library that Ashurbanipal's wife, like Nebuchadnezzar's in the account of Diodorus, missed her mountainous homeland with its verdant forests, so her husband had an artificial mountain built for her in Nineveh. Diodorus says the Babylonian queen was from the land of the Medes (Zagros Mountains) and elsewhere says that Semiramis was the mythical queen who built the walls of Babylon, but his texts are often confused. For more evidence at Nineveh, there are at least fifty holes on one side of the top of Kuyunjik mound in Nineveh that have been interpreted as artificial root ball sockets for imported tree plantings. Furthermore, remains of the Ninevite canals and aqueducts are still visible, bringing water from the mountains of Kurdistan to the north, channels that in some cases stretch for almost forty miles.

My own personal involvement in this story is small but interesting to relate. When I was a postdoctoral research fellow working with David Stronach at Berkeley around 1992–94, he had me involved in various stone-related assignments, including stone provenance (looking for geological sources of archaeological stone) and photogrammetry assessments of the 1989–90 Berkeley excavations of Nineveh. David Stronach is frequently acknowledged to be one of the world's preeminent archaeologists of the twentieth century, so I was fortunate to be able to learn directly from him. I'll never forget sessions with Stronach at his home along with Mark Hall, another research fellow, when we spent some time examining maps and aerial surveys of the remnant walls of Nineveh, comparing 1958 British Royal Air Force aerial photographs around Mosul, in which the walls were still very much visible against the bare land, with new panchromatic GIS satellite maps. Using stereoscopic glasses on parallel photos makes flat features pop out in relief. Employing both old aerial photos and new satellite imagery together can result in a good symbiosis for topographic analyses.

On the mound of Kuyunjik I noticed fascinating infrared data on the west side where a close-up of reflected infrared light—compared to the old RAF aerial photos for a baseline—showed that the material of the mound itself contained many types of different composite materials, most likely soils for special plant habitats. My minimal work as a team member of the postexcavation research at Nineveh suggests that some portion of Kuyunjik was augmented with artificial or special soils for first Sennacherib's and then Ashurbanipal's gardens. David Stronach and now others have not challenged Herodotus and Diodorus Siculus on whether such marvelous hanging gardens existed but merely raised the question of where they originated. Unlike the site of Babylon, which was buried but never completely forgotten, the rediscovery of Nineveh around 1850 still raises enormous implications: not only is it possible that Nineveh instead of Babylon was responsible for this wonder of the ancient world, but there may yet be undiscovered stories and forgotten histories recorded and waiting to be found in the now accessible texts of the Assyrian library at Nineveh.

Conclusion

The same fire in 612 BC that destroyed the city of Nineveh also baked the clay tablets of the Assyrian library, preserving them for 2,500 years until 1850. This collection of some twenty-six thousand clay tablet fragments, now mostly at the British Museum, tell us more about Mesopotamian life than any other single source. The story is filled with intrigue and perspicacity, courage and hardship, all because resourceful and intrepid individuals like Austen Henry Layard, Henry Rawlinson, Hormuzd Rassam, George Smith, David Stronach and many others, including Mesopotamian scholars like Irving Finkel, John Curtis and their museum colleagues in London, all wanted to know more about ancient Mesopotamia. These individuals, spread out over the last few centuries, refused to let a difficult region of the Near East and a daunting script from antiquity stand in the way of a greater understanding of the past.

Chapter 4

King Tut's Tomb
The Key to Egypt's God-Kings

Valley of the Kings, Egypt, 1922

Even in late November, an intense desert heat that was stored underground also filled the darkness that had been concealing deep secrets for millennia. Sweat soaked the shirts of the men who were trying to keep the dust out of their eyes and lungs. They were impatient with their slow progress and were worn down from day after day of removing rubble from the long tunnel seemingly reluctant to be cleared. Whoever had filled the stairways and chambers so many ages past had wanted it to be an undisturbed resting place and eternally safe from tomb robbers. Now the moment had finally come to break through the last barrier of bricked-up wall. The hubbub of echoing voices that had relayed muted instructions suddenly hushed altogether as every eye peered and no one breathed for a moment. With a softly scraping sigh, the last brick and mortar tumbled inward and a black hole appeared amid the dust. When his beam of light passed through the settling dust, a gasp was heard from Howard Carter. The light reflected back from polished gold everywhere; the gleaming sight almost stopped his heart.

In 1922, Howard Carter's astonished eyes were the first to witness the intact grandeur of an Egyptian pharaoh for almost 3,400 years, and Carter will be forever attached to his discovery of Tut's tomb. In a combination of dogged persistence and rare good luck, Carter was able to achieve a dream that few are even able to consider. After five long frustrating years, from 1918 onward, in his active search for this one elusive tomb—the last of the Egyptian pharaohs to be accounted for—Carter was able to use practical logic to pin down the most probable location. This was because the rest of the space in the Valley of the Kings was crowded with other royal tombs from the New Kingdom's prior and succeeding dynasties. Since no one had ever found Tutankhamun's resting place, nor had any of his grave goods ever surfaced in known history, Carter was convinced the tomb existed. Although Tut was not even important enough to make the Egyptian king list known from Greco-Roman times, Carter suspected this was due to the upheavals of civil war. All this mystery fed Carter's hope that he could locate an intact tomb with a sealed treasure, unheard of in Egyptian circles, since almost all had been robbed out millennia ago. What silent tombs remained in the valley were barren of their once fabulous wealth. Had Carter even found an empty tomb clearly identifiable as Tut's with hieroglyphic royal inscriptions, that would have been satisfaction enough for most archaeologists. But instead he found untold pharaonic wealth in a boy king's forgotten tomb and Carter himself became instantly famous. We can ask why King Tutankhamun's tomb discovery was so earthshaking, and here are some likely answers.

King Tut's tomb is the most spectacular archaeological find of the twentieth century, and the tomb contents and sarcophagus are the richest to have survived from ancient Egypt, as these treasures fill an entire wing of the Egyptian Museum in Cairo. The dramatic discovery was made more rewarding by Howard Carter's earlier failures. After decades of study, Tut's traveling exhibitions since the 1970s have drawn more visitors than any other museum event and Tut's tomb has stimulated "Egyptomania" more than anything else from Egypt has—millions of people worldwide instantly recognize Tut's golden death mask. Yet, despite all that we can discover today by modern science, the mystery surrounding Tut's death continues to invite enormous speculation and contributes to his allure.

These are only a few of the most important reasons why King Tut's tomb and its contents have made such a lasting impression on the world since 1922. The story is a dramatic saga, so we will look at excerpts of the discovery in Carter's own words. While archaeologists might find added reasons to list this discovery as perhaps the most important of the past century or so, it is probably more a popular choice than a scholarly one. Nonetheless it is hard to argue against, since Tut's name is one of the most famous in modern history, heavily influencing our understanding of ancient Egypt. The greatest irony in this discovery is our realization of how little impact he made in his own time. Proof of this is demonstrated by how quickly his name and tomb were lost, which is astonishing to anyone who has seen Tut's treasures.

A tomb is sealed, 1323 BC

Long ago, in the year now known as 1323 BC, a small procession wound its way quietly at sunset through the Valley of the Kings. The Egyptian horizon still glowed gold and pink from the sun but the sky was rapidly turning from turquoise to purple. The prayers to the gods were almost finished and all that remained were a few ceremonies and the sealing of the tomb. It would be sacrilege to dishonor the gods with excessive noise, so the group of workers and priests observed silence as they walked carefully down the cut stone steps into the tomb. The priests were to place the last food offerings and make final prayers, and the workers were to move some heavy gold objects and a few other sacred relics before they filled around the tomb door with rubble and then placed hard limestone seals around the underground lintel. Descending in their linen loincloths, the workers had to blink their eyes in the diminished light. The torches held above the shaved heads of the priests flickered in the dark tomb as they surveyed the spread of riches stacked up in orderly fashion around the hastily cut rock. The priests first counted and recorded all the items in the tomb, directing the workmen to move and rearrange many inventoried objects. All could see that the unseemly chisel marks could not be disguised or plastered and painted over with traditional scenes of blessing. A few of them, those who had family members working as craftsmen in the workers' village on the western bank of the river, knew it had all been done too quickly.

The royal tomb was astonishingly small, hardly befitting a god-king pharaoh as all of them knew, but then this boy king had not ruled long and, through no fault of his own, had many enemies. The priests made a few final sacrifices and offerings, singing songs that were spells to protect the dead. The standing workers waited, quietly looking on in approval at the centerpiece of the tomb, the king's triple-nested stone sarcophagus with its outermost cover hiding the gleaming gold underneath. Deep inside this stone sarcophagus they knew his embalmed mummy lay unmoving, although they could not see it. It had taken seventy days to embalm the dead boy king, after which the intricate coffin had swallowed him up, with its three enclosing cases, each elaborate and priceless after months of craftsmanship by the royal artisans, gold workers, enamel workers, stoneworkers and many more. The silent onlookers knew his mummy was guarded against decay with endless layers of wrapped linen soaked in natron. Sewn into this fine royal linen of the dead young pharaoh's mummy casing were hundreds of tiny amulets carved in precious stone, protecting the body against all kinds of disasters not covered by embalming.

The workers' eyes scanned across the several chambers, seeing his great gilded couches for resting and the huge gilded shrine with intricate scenes, so tall it almost touched the rough-hewn rock ceiling, topped by gold cobras with their flared hoods. While other shrine scenes in the tomb gave promises of safety and strength for the dead boy king's passage through the underworld, this one had magnificent gold scenes of the boy king and his family in happier days that surely would return in his afterlife. The four figures of the great golden goddesses, Isis, Nephthys, Selkis and Neith, faced inward with outstretched arms in all four directions, and the workmen knew that inside their chest shrine were the king's canopic jars in which his entrails soaked in oil, palm wine and natron. Over there was his royal chariot with its polished and gilded wood, ready for hunting in the afterlife. Everywhere was ivory, gold, blue-green faience and painted wood. The eleven great oars for moving his underworld boat were placed along the northern wall. A brightly painted ivory chest was decorated with hunting scenes. All around were stacked fine carved alabaster vessels and golden cups for enjoying the afterlife. This boy king and god, albeit a lesser one compared to his many predecessors, would be sent off in fitting style to the afterlife.

The priests finished their last rituals amid clouds of incense, signaling it was time to leave the tomb and seal the inner chamber. Their last glimpse was of the eyes of the vigilant linen-wrapped statuary sled of Anubis, the jackal-headed god who protected the cemeteries. Then the workmen sealed the door with plaster, over which the priests added more seals. It took many hours after that to move blocks of stone and rubble into the corridor, but they had nearly all night. They were all thankful to have seen the wonders and treasures inside the tomb, visions that would remain with them for the rest of their lives. When they at last filled in the great outer door and plastered it as well, the priests added final seals and the stairway cut down into the rock was filled with stone, mud and sand, step by step until it was flush with the floor of the valley. They stamped their feet over and over to compact it, then threw sand over it to cover it completely. The stars were blazing overhead in the middle of the night when they finished. The procession left the valley under starlight in the same silence they had entered with, for this was a sacred place.

This event over three thousand years ago was somehow remarkably forgotten, as was the tomb location of one of Egypt's most minor and short-lived kings. In the civil war that followed King Tutankhamun's death, his memory was hardly worth keeping as new dynasties struggled for control. Later kings like the far greater Rameses family ruled, and members of this dynasty put tomb workers' huts right over the forgotten and buried doorway to King Tut's tomb. A few grave robbers had entered the tomb at some point, strewing some of the contents and seemingly leaving just as hastily in fear. These robbers had probably come not long after the tomb was sealed, possibly led by some of the less reverent workers or even priests who had seen it sealed. The bulk of the treasure of King Tut's tomb waited millennia to be rediscovered, so it did not share the same fate as nearly every other royal tomb, all of them larger and more elegant, carved and finished over the lifetimes of their eventual occupants, but nearly always robbed and emptied out within a few centuries of their construction. It appears that there were cynical unbelievers even in ancient Egypt, possibly even among the ruling class or the priests. Either grave robbers did not fear tomb curses or they knew there would be no revenge from defunct dynasties that had no descendants to protect them. Tut's tomb escaped that typical fate because of civil war and general instability.

King Tut's tomb is the most spectacular archaeological find of the twentieth century

Although many modern archaeology finds deserve mention, none compares to the story of Howard Carter's search and the drama of his discovery. In addition, the sheer value of the grave goods in Tut's tomb exceeds all other finds. Then there is the lure of Egyptomania, a topic whose magnetic appeal reaches around the globe, not only to people of all ages but to all time. Part of the attraction is Egypt itself, but here it is coupled with the mystery of Tut's life and death. Much of the academic world was surprised at Howard Carter's tenacity and faith in his search when many others would have given up under such unpromising circumstances. The fact that this is the rarest of tombs to have survived intact at all only adds to the spectacular nature of Carter's quest. Conventionally, the tomb is named KV 62 after its location in the Valley of the Kings (KV) and its number 62, which cannot nearly convey the legendary lure. Although only a few years ago another tomb was discovered nearby, named KV 64, its contents are relatively poor and fragmentary since it was mostly emptied out like so many others or used merely for storage.

Among the many amazing elements in the spectacle of Tut's tomb, first is that although all the gold is no doubt beautiful to look at, very few realize how very hard the sarcophagus is, carved from quartzite, the hardest stone the Egyptians traditionally worked. The Egyptians didn't have steel and this stone is harder than steel. So the staggering amount of work to carve a huge stone box almost nine feet long and then decorate it with figures at the corners is compounded by the quartzite being so very hard. This was not possible to do quickly, so the work may have been started at Tut's accession to the throne as pharaoh when he was around sixteen years old. Second, many precious objects in the tomb actually belonged to his family predecessors like the heretic king Akhenaten. These objects tell us much about these family members' wealth and power as well, remarkable because the Theban priesthood of Amun had destroyed most of Akhenaten's city, Amarna, and his personal material goods.

Third, the inventory of items must represent a fairly complete set of royal tomb goods only a god-king of Egypt could expect in order to secure a better afterlife. There are so many hundreds of religious objects imbued with afterlife "magic" power that we can much better understand Egyptian religion from a royal perspective. In this case, however, nearly every object is made of precious or semiprecious material, which the Egyptian commoner could never afford. Fourth, because mention of triple-nested coffins is rare even in documents, finding one intact is almost beyond belief. This is especially relevant because in addition to the immensely hard quartzite stone sarcophagus cover, the two outer coffins are made of gilded wood, whereas the innermost coffin is of the purest solid gold. Fifth, few people realize that Howard Carter also excavated Thutmose IV's tomb (KV 43) in 1903. Although it had been heavily looted and the grave goods were damaged and incomplete, it had enough pharaonic artifacts (for example, a carved-relief throne and carved chariot of decorated wood with stucco) that Carter knew what sort of objects he might expect to encounter in a previously unknown tomb like Tut's, one that he hoped had not been systematically emptied by looting. Sixth, the wide range of materials used in Tut's tomb not only provides great insight into Egyptian crafts of the time and includes gold, silver, electrum (gold-silver alloy) ivory, faience, turquoise, blue lapis lazuli, carnelian, glass, woods (including cedar, ebony and others), textile (mostly fine linen) and many other materials, but also showcases the royal consumption of luxury goods. Some of these rare and beautiful stones are so hard as to require labor-intensive craftsmanship. Thus, despite the fact that he was a poor king in a turbulent period, we learn an enormous amount about ancient Egypt and its god-kings through what was preserved in Tut's tomb.

The tomb and sarcophagus are the richest to have survived from Egypt, possibly anywhere

No one has yet been able to give an exact value of the wealth in Tutankhamun's tomb. The estimates must run in astronomical figures because of the materials used and their quantity, but we can try to understand this value by comparing Tut's tomb to today's standards. For gold alone, some economic historians have attempted to add up the inner solid gold coffin, the amazing objects like solid gold sandals, the gilded shrines and the hundreds of objects like shoulder pectoral collars, rings, necklaces, statuettes, scepters and myriad other pieces of jewelry, not even counting the religious paraphernalia. To evaluate it we'd need to separate the intrinsic from extrinsic value—impossible at the outset—but we can at least look at a few tangible components of that wealth.

An extremely conservative estimate of the gold in Tut's tomb must start somewhere around 2,500 pounds of very pure gold (his inner coffin alone would probably weigh at least 2,000 pounds). Gold is usually weighed in troy ounces and there are 14.6 troy ounces to a normal (avoirdupois) pound. If gold in 2007 is worth an inflated $650 an ounce (that is, a troy ounce) and there are 14.6 troy ounces in a normal pound, then the net value of gold alone in Tut's tomb would currently be worth somewhere around $23.7 million (650 times 14.6 times 2,500), using current gold bullion market standards. We must remember this is a very conservative estimate based on raw gold bullion value alone. We add in inflation today when we calculate the value of gold, but in antiquity gold prices better reflected the scarcity of this rare and extremely precious metal.

Fort Knox, the U.S. federal treasury repository for gold, does not actually verify its listed total gold reserves, but we can assume it is listed somewhere as around 9 million pounds. Without factoring in historic perspectives, this Fort Knox volume may make King Tut's gold seem paltry, since until recent times gold in individual circulation usually exceeded any national treasury unless there were sumptuary laws prohibiting commoners to own gold (which was frequently the case). In reality, by comparing the smaller volume of gold available in antiquity than today, Tut's tomb represents a larger fraction of the gold in circulation in Egypt and the world around 1323 BC, especially given that Egypt was the land of gold in the eyes of the ancient world and gold was religiously symbolic of the flesh of the gods. The pure gold circulating in the ancient world at that time was less than 25 percent of today's volume, because much more gold has been mined since 1325 BC and gold mining techniques have advanced in these subsequent thousands of years. All these calculations suggest that the gold in Tut's tomb would have been far more precious in 1323 BC than today because it was a much scarcer entity even in Egypt, the Land of Gold.

Of course, the arbitrary value assigned to Tut's tomb gold doesn't even count the other precious materials (for example, silver, carnelian, lapis lazuli, turquoise, ivory, alabaster, diorite porphyry and other hard stones, ebony wood and so on), nor does it count the extrinsic value of the highest royal craftsmanship or the priceless value of intact and beautifully crafted antiquities themselves thousands of years old. Even a genuine but rather ordinary clay pot from this Egyptian Eighteenth Dynasty period would fetch thousands of dollars at antiquities auction prices. Any inventory of other objects from Tut's tomb would be even more inflated in value just because the source was Tut's tomb (of course, none of these Tutankhamun items are for sale anyway so it's a specious argument). But the only conclusion we can arrive at about the astonishing economic value of Tut's tomb is absolute pricelessness. No wonder that traveling exhibitions of even small portions of King Tut's tomb collection have to be insured to the hilt.

Whatever else we could say about the treasure in Tut's tomb, it provides our first and only material basis for a measure of pharaonic wealth. If Tut was a poor minor pharaoh who ruled for only a few years in the New Kingdom, we can only imagine how much personal wealth powerful rulers like Rameses II or Thutmose could have accrued. In the case of Rameses, it would likely be even more staggering because he ruled for fifty-five years. In this one aspect and in so many other ways, Tut's tomb has opened our eyes to a whole new understanding of the god-kings of Egypt and their fabulous wealth. No wonder either that nearly all the other tombs were robbed so often by their successors, given the treasures that were simply waiting to be taken with little to no resistance. Most of the law-abiding Egyptians appear to have believed that if they robbed the graves and the death penalty didn't get them in this life, the religious penalties and eternal retribution would catch them in the next life. It seems the pharaohs themselves worried little about either penalty, but instead relied on magic from their priests, on amulets like their heart scarabs, along with the armies they controlled, to protect them.

Howard Carter's earlier failures made the dramatic discovery more rewarding

Before 1922 Howard Carter's life was a series of ups and downs, and he was greatly frustrated over the elusive tomb he sought. The previous six years had turned up nothing but dust. That he was well prepared for his task was certain, but his luck had not always been dependable.

Howard Carter (1874–1939) trained as an artist and draftsman before coming under the lure of Egyptology. Carter first went to Egypt in 1891, at age eighteen, where he was personally under the tutelage of the greatest British archaeologist of his day, William Matthew Flinders Petrie (1853–1942), often said to be the "Father of Modern Egyptology" and later knighted in 1923. Because Petrie had an extensive background in civil engineering survey techniques from his father, a surveyor (although his grandfather was a famous explorer and sea captain), Carter learned much from Petrie about combining the accurate eye of the artist with the quantitative measurements of an engineer. Carter rapidly rose to secure an expatriate position through the Egypt Exploration Fund and became a chief inspector for the Egyptian Antiquities Service at a time when the British controlled much of Egypt's administration. He even excavated Thutmose IV's tomb in 1903 in the Valley of the Kings, so he knew it as well as anyone. But in 1905 Carter had a run-in with French tourists and it ended disastrously, with a forced resignation and humiliating years of living hand to mouth while pursuing his passion for Egyptology. Working as a guide and freelance archaeologist, Carter met George Herbert, Lord Carnarvon, who was convalescing in Egypt. Carnarvon shared Carter's passion for Egypt and soon became his sponsor. During World War I, when few archaeologists were working in Egypt, Lord Carnarvon obtained an excavation permit in 1917 through his ample British connections. This permit, for a project in the Valley of the Kings, allowed him to underwrite Carter's first search for Tut's tomb. It was a bleak six years as Carter, despite his good training, scoured the valley floor back and forth with many anguishing false starts.

Lord Carnarvon was going to pull the plug on fruitless funding when Carter persuaded him to fund one last season. Carter arrived back in Egypt on October 28, 1922, and was hard at work trying to end his archaeological drought. Everything changed on November 4. Carter had instructed his workers to go back to a spot they had previously examined without much attention since it was covered by workers' huts for a later and grander tomb, that of Rameses VI of the Twentieth Dynasty. On this day, only four days into the dig, to the growing excitement of Carter, his workers quickly took down the mud brick huts' haphazard foundations and soon found the first step leading to a hidden sunken doorway just off the valley floor in an unimposing corner. Carter immediately noticed that this doorway was not on any maps or archived site plans, and he instructed his workers to continue at a feverish pace, uncovering the full rock-cut passage within a few days down to the twelfth step in the rock. He now knew it had to be a tomb, and a previously unknown one at that. He desperately hoped it would be intact, which would be a miracle, or at least sufficiently covered with inscriptions to prove its owner. The priestly seals he found proved it was a tomb for a high personage, possibly even a royal tomb.

In the interim, on November 6, Carter had contacted Lord Carnarvon back in England and impatiently waited for the ship and his sponsor. When Lord Carnarvon landed in Alexandria on November 23, they hastily returned to Luxor and the Valley of the Kings. Together they oversaw the full excavation of the first door down to the sixteenth step. Now riveted at the fully exposed doorway, frantically whispering aloud as he traced the dusty hieroglyphs, this exact moment when Howard Carter discovered that this was the tomb of King Tut must go down in archaeology as the one of the most exciting events in our discipline. That Carter had spent blistering decades pondering and searching for this one tomb as his young life withered away under the merciless Egyptian sun made it all the more rewarding. This drama quickly unfolded a few days later during the most important day of his life when, after all the delaying passage-filling rubble and debris left behind the first door was removed, Carter and Lord Carnarvon finally arrived at the second door. With trembling hands and wildly thumping heart Carter poked through a corner in the dim light to peer into the darkness within. This is the moment of truth for an archaeologist, when time becomes eternity. In Howard Carter's own words, written in 1923, we can read his memory of November 26, 1922:

The decisive moment had arrived. With trembling hands I made a tiny breach in the upper left-hand corner. Darkness and blank space, as far as the iron testing rod could reach, showed that whatever lay beyond was empty and not filled like the passage we had just cleared. Candle tests were applied as a precaution against possible gases, and then, widening the hole a little, I inserted the candle and peered in . . . At first I could see nothing, the hot air escaping from the chamber causing the candle flame to flicker, but presently, as my eyes grew accustomed to the light, details of the room within emerged slowly from the mist, strange animals, statues, and gold—everywhere the glint of gold. For a moment—an eternity it must have seemed to the others standing by—I was struck dumb with amazement, and when Lord Carnarvon, unable to stand the suspense any longer, inquired anxiously, "Can you see anything?" it was all I could do to get out the words, "Yes, wonderful things."

The gleam of gold reflected everywhere in the light must have nearly stopped Howard Carter's heart as he croaked out the dusty words that have become the most famous in archaeology. The dense complexity of the treasures within took ten years to fully excavate and even longer to inventory. They are still being studied in 2007 and will be for years to come.

Tut's tomb riches fill an entire wing of the Egyptian Museum

Visiting the Egyptian Museum in Cairo is an unforgettable experience. While it is not always comfortable (especially when there is no air conditioning—or air circulation—and the outside temperature is like a furnace), this does little to erode the visitor's amazement over King Tut's treasures, which fill an entire wing of the museum's extensive collection of antiquities. Consider that the objects on display, however poorly lit and crammed into cases, are only part of the total volume of materials Carter and Lord Carnarvon, among others, removed from the tomb over a ten-year period.

More Tut materials are stored in the basement vaults, and one can see in the museum that the objects that travel in exhibitions make up only a tiny fraction of the whole Tut collection. If the materials from Tut's tomb were displayed according to the less-crowded standards of European or American museums, they would nearly fill an entire museum of a large city.

Tut's traveling exhibitions have drawn more visitors than any other museum event

From 1976 to 1979, a blockbuster traveling King Tut exhibition across seven cities in the United States drew over 8 million visitors, not even counting schoolchildren and many free tickets. In 2005, twenty-six years later, a much smaller exhibition drew over 300,000 advance ticket buyers in Los Angeles alone and an expected revenue of over $100 million throughout the tour. An article in the *Los Angeles Times* (May 22, 2005) recorded that this same Tut traveling exhibition was seen by 620,000 people in Basel in 2004 and later by 870,000 at the Art and Exhibition Hall in Bonn, Germany.

A significant portion of the 2004–5 Tut traveling exhibition earnings are earmarked for conservation of the Egyptian Museum in Cairo, and archaeology officials in Egypt are expecting to receive around $7.7 million from each of its European cities. Egypt required a ticket sale guarantee of $6 million from each U.S. city before even committing to the exhibition, and these proceeds are to be used for reinvigorating modern archaeology in Egypt. In all the clamor of publicity and inevitable long lines at many traveling exhibitions, one thing is certain: Tut has been outdrawing all other popular draws, including the impressionists and other great masters. A much-acclaimed 1999 Van Gogh exhibition in Los Angeles drew 821,000 visitors, and was considered a blockbuster; in comparison, a large display of Tut objects drew over 1,250,000 visitors in 1978, and a much smaller group of Tut objects drew at least a million visitors in 2005.

Tut's tomb has stimulated Egyptomania more than anything else from Egypt has

While popular interest in Tut has never claimed to be academic, Egyptomania since the discovery of Tut has flourished. Terry Garcia, an executive of the National Geographic Society, says that the society has had a strong focus on Egypt for over a century. "The number one topic we have published in all these years has been Egypt, more than any of the ones we've done work on in 116 years of our existence," Garcia stated at the Los Angeles County Museum of Art during the 2005 Tut exhibit.

In 1963, Elizabeth Taylor starred in the mega box office epic *Cleopatra*, which has since been billed as "the film that changed Hollywood." But the popularity and impact of this memorable film itself grew on the earlier media sensation of Howard Carter's 1922 discovery. Tut's popularity continues in the media today, including silly cinema burlesques or caricatures of archaeology such as the *Tomb Raider* movies (2001, 2003) and the

Mummy movies (1999, 2001). Modern viewers either forget or never knew that these remakes owe much to classics like Boris Karloff's *The Mummy* (1932), its timing directly spawned by Carter's discovery. Perhaps the most endearing spoof of Tut comes from the wonderful Belgian classic comic hero Tintin in Hergé's *Cigars of the Pharaoh* (*Les Cigares du Pharaon*) released in 1934, again a direct response to the lionizing of Howard Carter's excavation in the Valley of the Kings. Some slyly suggest that Egyptology is merely an educated person's Egyptomania, but it might just as easily be said that Egyptology is professional Egyptomania.

Millions of people worldwide instantly recognize Tut's golden death mask

That one of the most recognizable icons of the twentieth century is Tut's familiar golden death mask, with its blue and gold stripes across the headdress, speaks volumes for Tut's influence. A pair of obsidian eyes lined in jeweled imitation kohl track the viewer everywhere. These riveting eyes are set in a face reflecting a fabulous golden light around an imperturbable mouth that wears the weight of divine kingship, neither smiling or frowning but merely acknowledging the outside world. Its association with death makes it even more widely popular, as it fuses several fascinations or taboos. This is a remarkable visage, given that its owner never reached the ripe old age of nineteen.

Tut's golden death mask is a perfect popular vehicle for condensing information about archaeology and ancient history. Icons like this help museums to secure more public sponsorship for curation and research in ancient history. Since early education in childhood prepares the general public for later willingness to underwrite such museum sponsorship, even schoolchildren need images like Tut's mask that conjure up the past. Many archaeologists outside Egyptology often refer to popular fascination with King Tut as "Tutmania" and the "Tut Glut," usually more sarcastically than fondly. Yet the fact remains that archaeology requires constant public support; it is a discipline dependent on sometimes tedious and repetitive quantitative analytical methods and therefore is an expensive field of study in constant need of funding. So we professional archaeologists should not bite the hand that feeds us. If the public wants more information on Tut, this will in turn cross-fertilize other archaeology and help maintain general research. Tut's iconic golden face has single-handedly done a lot for archaeology.

The mystery surrounding Tut's death continues to invite enormous speculation

He reigned for a very short time, possibly only five to nine years, but speculation about King Tut's death has been rampant since the original X-rays seemed to show head fractures and bone splinters at the back of his skull. In his well-written 1998 book, *The Murder of King Tutankhamen: A True Story*, Bob Brier of Long Island University describes Tut's death as murder, and he carefully sets out the likely motives, culprits and methods like a forensic CSI detective. However, recent CAT scans (made in 2005) have greatly modified some of these suggested traumas. Funded in part by the National Geographic Society and Siemens Medical Solutions of Germany, using state-of-the-art analytical instruments, the noninvasive imaging involved up to 1,700 images, even though not all scholars agree they are definitive. From these CAT scans, we can see that Tut's skeleton appears to show a very bad leg fracture, which may have gone septic into a fatal infection, as was common in antiquity from wounds and infections.

Because the Carter excavations did significant damage to Tut's remains, separating the deceased young king's body into sections and probing it for other details, it is very difficult to distinguish modern disarticulation of bones from the ancient embalming process, let alone determining exact cause of death. The 3,400 intervening years have also somewhat muted the evidence.

Many questions surround Tut's reign. He is not named in the incomplete Turin King List (primarily because it stops at the Seventeenth Dynasty, around 1700 BC, and Tut was a late Eighteenth Dynasty king), nor is he or his likely father Akhenaten recorded in the great Abydos King List recorded by Seti, who founded the next great dynasty (Ramessides) after Tut, around 1300 BC. The other king list, from the Ptolemaic Greek period, was compiled by Manetho in 271 BC and also omits Tut, along with others such as Tut's enigmatic relative Akhenaten. Lack of documentation about Tut's life still leaves us unsatisfied as to whether he was really a son of Akhenaten by Kiya, a minor wife. Speculation continues over whether Tut was married to a daughter of Akhenaten whose name was originally Ankhesenaten but was changed to Ankhesenamun, for reasons explained below. This would make Tut's young adolescent wife also a half sister, not unheard of in Egyptian royal families of the New Kingdom.

Akhenaten had a lot of enemies, especially the powerful Theban priesthood of Amun. Tut was most likely born at Amarna, Akhenaten's new capital, around 1340 BC but had a different name at birth: Tutankhaten, not Tutankhamun. Like his wife's name, his was changed possibly in fear and definitely to dissociate him from Akhenaten. When the Theban priesthood reasserted itself in the unstable period around the time of Tut's death, it destroyed Akhenaten's city of Amarna and everything associated with it. Tut's successors, first his military relative Ay, who was associated with the Theban priests, and then General Horemheb, suggest to many that foul play was involved in his death at the highest level of the Egyptian hierarchy. But if the new CAT scans of Tut's mummy are more definitive, his young death may not be so suspicious. We may never know because this transitional period is not well documented due to Egyptian instability. Since speculation abounds where evidence is lacking, Tut's life and death will probably always remain somewhat elusive, and this mystery will likely make him even more attractive in the future.

Conclusion

The greatest irony about Tutankhamun is that his tomb, paradoxically loaded with lavish treasures but crudely unfinished, has elevated him to superstar status in the modern world, when he hardly made a blip in ancient Egypt. This treasure and its discovery ranks as one of the greatest stories in the world, and by it a minor pharaoh has been transformed into a figure whose name is far more familiar than any of his predecessors and successors whose power and impact on their own worlds were exponentially greater. This is one of the caprices of history but cannot undermine why Tut has done so much more for history and archaeology in his once-forgotten death than in his short forgotten life. For Tut, like all Egyptian pharaoh god-kings who lived for eternity more than the present, this may be the most fitting justice.

Chapter 5

Machu Picchu
The Key to Inca Architecture

Peruvian High Jungle, 1916

The humid landscape seemed to climb ever upward as Hiram Bingham's eyes tried to gauge how high the mountain jungle's vertical peaks pierced the mists and clouds around him. He hardly dared to look down where the precipice dropped to frothy rapids raging thousands of feet below. He and his guide had been ascending for hours, wet branches dripping over them because there was no real trail through the steep twisting terrain; instead, they'd turn first this direction, then that, on endless switchbacks hacked open by the guide's machete. Bingham's guide hardly ever spoke, but they shared a grudging respect for each other. The short Quechua farmer never seemed out of breath, perfectly at ease in climbing practically straight up and sometimes hand over fist, as each man had to pull himself upward. Bingham, on the other hand, was tall and lanky, but hard and fit after a few seasons exploring South America on foot and by mule.

The Quechua man pointed up ahead, only nodding with a wordless toothy smile in his earthy brown face that was the color of clay. Bingham now saw the steepest climb up ahead, almost touching the clouds, and before turning away, his guide squeezed Bingham's arm, then pinched his thumb to his index finger to indicate the universal sign of only a little way yet to go. Bingham sighed and pushed his heavy, aching legs the last bit until the ridge suddenly leveled and fell away under them, revealing an amazing sight at the top of the narrow mountain. Hiram Bingham let out a low whistle, as intricately wrought terrace after stone terrace filled his whole vista. Who could have guessed that there was a whole lost city hidden away on the top of this mountain, one where the jungle had long overtaken these breathtaking walls that reached the sky? The Quechua guide nodded at Bingham's amazement, and merely uttered what Bingham thought were magic words: "Machu Picchu."

Why Machu Picchu?

If any archaeological site in the world evokes awe and mystery, Machu Picchu is it, as it sits literally on top of the world. Machu Picchu is a magnet to thousands of first-time visitors each year. Some people even travel to Peru and the towering Andes just to glimpse Machu Picchu, and tourists usually outnumber archaeologists by at least a thousand to one. Peruvians had even declared that Machu Picchu should be counted as one of the Seven Wonders of the World. In fact, by popular world vote in 2007, Machu Picchu is now listed as one of the new Seven Wonders of the World. So it is no surprise that global travelers most often list it first among their dream destinations. What is the mysterious source of attraction about Machu Picchu? Machu Picchu is one of the most spectacular places in the world, by design, as it is also one of the most perfect examples of dramatic Inca landscape architecture and incredible stoneworking genius. Its deliberate isolation, in steeply remote mountains—and its location kept secret from Spanish conquistadores—combined with political and cultural differences between highland and lowland Peru, helped preserve Machu Picchu's secrets for hundreds of years. While still only a legend, Machu Picchu became the focus of Hiram Bingham's search as an intrepid explorer. And it's full of surprises—researches have recently discovered that Machu Picchu's artisan/builders used acoustic engineering in ways previously unthinkable.

Ask anyone who is adventurous and has a list of must-see places in the world this question: If you haven't already been to South America, what place there do you most dream of visiting? Of anyone who has even a glimmer of interest in history, seven out of ten immediately respond, "Machu Picchu." This figure comes from IATA (International Association of Travel Agents) surveys of travel operators and tour groups as well as adventure surveys. Why is Machu Picchu so important and why does it dominate this collective "must-see" list? Part of the answer is fairly straightforward and part is not so obvious to nonarchaeologists and nonhistorians, but the fact that it is so magnetic and mysterious a place to both scholars and intrepid adventurers is exactly the point, and possibly why the Inca created Machu Picchu in the first place.

Machu Picchu is one of the most spectacular places in the world

All experienced travelers who see Machu Picchu agree it is one of the most spectacular places in the world, perched high on the cliffs above the whitewater rapids of the Urubamba River gorge yet still framed by the jagged peaks of the Andes above it. One of the first observations anyone makes on looking around is how dramatic the vistas are on all sides. It is the dizzying verticality of the site that immediately strikes you. A small terraced plateau is dwarfed by sheer peaks rising thousands of feet above and the Urubamba gorge plummeting far below. Most scholars now agree that this drama was an intentional feature of the most likely builder, the Inca emperor Pachacuti around 1450. There is little doubt that part of its impact derives from its deliberate placement on a vertical axis. It was meant to impress all.

Machu Picchu was "lost" for almost five hundred years because the Spanish conquistadores were either ignorant or deliberately kept unaware of its existence. Being mostly "forgotten" by the Peruvians was also guaranteed because it was far from accessible routes and surrounded by sheer peaks and densely jungled canyons with only whitewater rapids tumbling through its unnavigable valley. Thus, the city is also unique because it was not discovered or altered by the Spanish conquest.

Today there is debate on whether the people of Peru really ever "forgot" about it or if they just kept it secret. The truth probably lies somewhere in between. Its remoteness was probably intended either for secrecy or more likely as a defensive strategy: invaders seeking to attack Machu Picchu would hardly know it was there unless they came from above, itself a daunting prospect. The one access road dating from the period, now called the Inca Trail, winds around the back side of the ridge over a vertical granite cliff where the only passageway, which is single file, can be blocked by moving a portable "bridge" from the path. This bridge is now only timber planks that cross a deep abyss, a man-made cliff-hugging stone causeway built by the Inca in a place where a thousand-foot wall of stone looms overhead and another jungled precipice falls away below. Remove that temporary thirty-foot wooden plank link and the site of Machu Picchu is protected by its isolation. The upper gate to the city is in a formidable wall where, again deliberately, one views Huayna Picchu's sheer peak framed in the doorway above the site. This all adds to its magnetic appeal and enhances the mystique surrounding its status as a "lost" city. What seems more and more likely is that Machu Picchu was probably designed to be remote and difficult to find.

Machu Picchu is an example of the greatest Inca stoneworking genius

Historians know that when the Spanish conquered Peru under Francisco Pizarro between 1532–41, they immediately set about transforming the Inca cities under Spanish rule into Europeanized structures, so much was lost in Cuzco. Inca palaces not completely torn down became foundations for colonial residences. Inca sacred sites like the Coricancha temple or the Temple of the Sun in Cuzco became the mostly invisible heart of the Church of Santo Domingo. The sacred "Puma" shape of Cuzco and the four roads from the four corners of the world arriving at the "Navel of the World" are now mostly obscured by later colonial construction. But Machu Picchu did not suffer the same fate, no doubt partly due to its deliberate isolation on a vertical ridge above whitewater torrents.

Machu Picchu's dramatic grandeur, far more clear than at Cuzco or nearly all other Inca sites, demonstrates a natural philosophy whereby the Inca were clearly intending to showcase their integration of man-made adaptation with natural beauty as well as a power over nature by building a stone city where one would least expect it.

This city also provides the most complete example of Inca social and civic planning. At Machu Picchu, whole intact precincts of an Inca urban plan were untouched, quarters for clans (*ayllus*) and hierarchical structures and habitations interconnected by stone staircases carved from solid rock. Some of the stones in the Great Stairway have polygonal faces numbering up to twelve sides. Many of us have admired the breathtaking plunge of its hundreds of ordered agricultural terraces stepping down the nearly vertical slopes. Most of all, we have been speechless at Machu Picchu's staggering use of natural landscape as an architectural form. Peruvian archaeologists like Santiago Agurto Calvo have documented over thirty-seven types of different "looks" on an Inca stone surface. Here one sees masonry with a remarkable variety of carved edges, each face unique and immensely difficult to carve without metal tools (unusable regardless because the stone—basalt, andesite, diorite and granite—is as hard as steel or harder, and they didn't have steel!). Nearly all the stones of Machu Picchu touch perfectly, without any visible gaps (the proverbial knife blade cannot penetrate between these stones), and the Inca would not simply place a six-sided block on top of another; they were more likely to carve a stone ashlar (a squarish "block") with unusual angles, flanges and crenellated edges. Plus, Machu Picchu itself was entirely quarried or carved out of the granite bedrock of this high site for economizing the immense labor of stone transport. The stone used at Machu Picchu had to travel hardly more than a half mile. With its perfectly designed location carved out of a mountain summit, midway between towering peaks above and vertiginous precipices below, Machu Picchu best represents the Inca philosophy of landscape use in a culture where nature itself was the most important part of the landscape and where human alteration was harmoniously integrated into nature. All of this taken together was a prodigious feat, most likely intended to impress then, just as it still does now.

The "mystery" of Machu Picchu still acts as a magnet, although *mystery* is often a byword for ignorance. Many archaeologists and historians now think Machu Picchu appears not to have been well known even to the remnant indigenous people of Peru during the suppressions and massacres of the Spanish conquest, led by Pizarro and his successors following 1541. If the Spanish had found out about Machu Picchu's existence, they would surely have uncovered its location—possibly through the well-known torture practiced by the Office of the Inquisition, intent on subjugating the Inca empire and taking away as much of its gold and silver as possible for "God, King and Country." Odd rumors still surface today about the quiet disappearances of adventurers searching for lost or hidden Inca treasure. The dangers of the terrain can be intimidating, where one misstep leads to certain death, plunging hundreds of feet from narrow paths clinging to cliffs, combined with venomous snakes and a hundred other dangers. Those who wander into uncharted territory looking for secret treasure are not so likely to return from this vertical terrain. But the persistence of stories of such disappearances suggests to some that zealous descendants of the proud Inca still fiercely guard their secrets.

Regional differences between highland and lowland Peru helped preserve Machu Picchu

On the other hand, regional politics in Peru play a role that is highlighted by the mountainous terrain. I and other archaeologists have also discovered the sometimes frustrating differences between the postcolonial lowlands and the mostly indigenous highlands. Opposition in the indigenously peopled highlands around Cuzco and Arequipa toward policy legislated in the "colonial" capital of Lima can also stymie archaeological research when politics intervene. Having a permit to conduct archaeological research written and stamped in Lima may not sit well in Cuzco, long presided over by a Marxist-leaning regime sometimes violently at odds with the national government.

I well remember a ferocious gun battle in 1988 at the bridge over the Urubamba River at Pisac where we'd seen the local police, the Guardia Civil, preparing for an impending attack by the Sendero Luminoso. We drove over the protected bridge guarded by rifle-bearing police behind sandbag barriers but we were high above the city on the ridge examining the Inca ruins when we later heard the gunfire reverberating below as the expected attack came. It was our reminder of a continuing struggle. Modern communication and emergency health services are sadly lacking. There is almost a complete absence of any hospitals or trained doctors over thousands of square miles. It is often still quite difficult to travel over such remote highland areas. Furthermore, intermittent lawlessness or political instability (such as was stirred up and utilized by the Sendero Luminoso, or "Shining Path" Maoists) against postcolonial landowners also fuels the rumors of disappearing treasure seekers. A natural suspicion of strangers, especially "gringos," is a local xenophobic response that can exacerbate the exploration problems those known to be foolishly seeking Inca gold may face. To some degree, it is likely that the indigenous people of the highlands and mountains have kept at bay the postcolonial world still dominated by old Spanish landowners, and this may have also helped to preserve Machu Picchu.

The modern Quechua descendants of the Inca are a highland people who will not easily forget the slavery and oppression brought by the colonial conquest. Incomplete documentation records that thousands of Quechua died in the seventeenth century, many enslaved deep in the silver mines of Oropesa. Meanwhile, various Vatican pontiffs debated the humanity of New World peoples and whether they had souls. Similar brutalities have been reported through the last few centuries over land dominance and slaughter of the Quechua when they protested or rebelled against such treatment. But in the case of Machu Picchu, its beauty and architectural wonders have only enhanced the modern world's admiration for the Inca and their enduring forbearance and stamina.

Bingham's 1911 discovery of this lost city made it possible for the first time to see what the fabulous Inca had secretly accomplished in these remotest of steep mountains, a high location above thick jungles that the Spanish conquistadores could never reach and destroy. Because of their isolation and secret location, these ruins were never changed and rebuilt by colonials to reflect European values; they remain striking examples of how the Inca lived before Columbus touched the New World.

To hide a whole city away so high over the whitewater rapids through the narrow jungle valleys, far from highly traveled routes, was ultimately a wise decision for world posterity. This region is part of what the Inca called Antisuyu, the rough land to the north of Cuzco, with its near impenetrable walls of steep cordillera.

Rumors of lost cities full of treasure plagued the Spanish, who spared no effort searching for them. Those in unhappy contact with the Spanish conquerors might possibly have known of and kept secret the existence of Machu Picchu, but it is unlikely that most of the indigenous Peruvians knew its location. Its exact purpose is still unknown—maybe it was a private royal city or a remote royal villa or even a strategic *qolqa* ("storehouse") where valued objects traded between the people of the mountains and the people of the jungles could be safely placed in transit while waiting for the next caravan of llamas to carry them onward in either direction. But the fact that it has important astronomical markers like the Intiwatana ("Hitching Post of the Sun") that line up at dawn with local peaks like Mount Salcantay and sun temples like the Torreón suggest other functions such as calendrical festivals and that it may have been a priestly center. Royal tombs under the Torreón could be interpreted as evidence that Machu Picchu was a sacred locale for the dynasty of Pachacuti, who built it. Hundreds of terraces for crops carved out and built into the cliffs, where aqueducts brought continuous water from higher up, prove Machu Picchu sustained intensive agriculture, leading historians to believe it was self-sufficient. All these different activities certainly require that Machu Picchu's exact purpose is yet to be carefully sought. Whatever its purposes, it remained hidden from the colonial powers for at least four centuries until around the beginning of the twentieth century. Fairly intrepid adventurers—now either on foot or by train and tour van— follow the footsteps of Inca llama caravans and later archaeologists to admire Machu Picchu's magnificence and its breathtaking vistas.

Machu Picchu before and after Hiram Bingham

Before considering Hiram Bingham's role in bringing Machu Picchu to light, it is important to consider what exploration may have preceded his dramatic visit. Several earlier European explorers and locals may have seen a bit of Machu Picchu before Bingham in 1911. Charles Wiener in 1880 had certainly heard of a lost mountain city in this region. Augustin Lizárraga knew of or sought a site above the jungle around 1899 or 1900 and may have even camped among the ruins without realizing how much lay underneath him. Two local Quechua villagers named Alvarez and Recharte apparently explored its agricultural terraces and may have even reused a fraction of them for a few years before Bingham arrived. But it is Hiram Bingham who placed Machu Picchu solidly on the world's consciousness with his rediscovery in 1911. He was in the company of a Quechua man named Arteaga who seemed to have camped across the river gorge from Machu Picchu in 1910 and therefore became Bingham's guide through this dangerous mountain region.

If there were ever a born explorer, Hiram Bingham fills those shoes. Few realize that the fictional character of Indiana Jones, archaeologist-explorer-adventurer extraordinaire, was most likely derived or modeled after Hiram Bingham. His family stock was *Mayflower* New Englanders, with famous names like Jonathan Brewster (1795–1865), his maternal grandfather, or the minister Hiram Bingham I (1789–1869), his paternal grandfather and namesake. Born of missionary parents in Hawaii in 1875, young Hiram Bingham III clambered up misty jungled peaks in Hawaii very similar to Peru's rain-clouded cliffs. One difference that perhaps stood out to the intrepid Bingham in 1911 was that, whereas native venomous snakes were unknown in Hawaii, in Peru he had to watch every step, not just slippery rocks but what crawled or slithered over them.

If there is an "exploring" gene somewhere yet undiscovered on the human genome map, Hiram Bingham must have possessed it. After a solid private school education and further privileged education at Yale, Harvard and Berkeley, Bingham appeared to be setting out on a worthy academic career. But first he needed some adventurous fieldwork to establish an academic reputation at Yale, where he was teaching as a junior faculty member. After taking part in the First Pan-American Scientific Congress in Santiago, Chile, in 1908, he decided to remain in South America to study the meandering routes of Simón Bolivar in his early-nineteenth-century independence journeys. He followed one leg of the long trip from Buenos Aires, Argentina, on his way to Lima, Peru. But he stopped somewhere in the middle, most likely Inca-rich Cuzco with its prolific Inca masonry, which still forms the foundations of this former capital city of a pre-Columbian empire. Cuzco was the once-proud navel of the Inca cosmos from which the four corners of the world spread out along its amazing road network. One road led west over the mountains to the Pacific coast; another led east to the green jungles; yet another went south to the Tiwanaku altiplano (a high plateau averaging over twelve thousand feet in elevation) and Lake Titicaca. The last road led north to what is now Ecuador and even Colombia. In Cuzco, after meeting with people like J. J. Nunez, who convinced him of the importance of the Inca, Bingham traded colonial history and the harsh thin Spanish overlay for the deeper undercurrent of older Inca lore. After hearing the story of the then lost city of Vilcabamba and seeing ruins in the region, Bingham heard rumors of another lost Inca city in the remote mountain jungles to the northeast and decided to search for it, abandoning all other research for the time being. He returned to the United States and Yale and then came back to Peru and assembled a team in 1911. This team included a police sergeant from Cuzco named Carrasco and intermediary guides, villagers who either knew of unmapped ruins or knew other distant villagers who would take him closer to the probable region.

His several-week journey involved going over the high Anta Plateau and down into the Yucay Valley by mule team, and finally hiking along the Urubamba gorge past Ollantaytambo. Bingham's team at last set up camp on July 23 at a place called Mandor Pampa, where the Urubamba River twists and turns almost a full circle through high granite peaks. Here a local farmer named Melchor Arteaga was curious about Bingham's search and either offered assistance for pay or was sought out because it was known he was farming in man-made ruined terraces on a high jungle plateau nearby that he called Machu Picchu. He translated this from his Quechua tongue as "Old Mountain," and above its ridge was a much higher jagged peak he called Huayna Picchu, or "New Mountain." Bingham wanted to explore the high unseen ruins early the next day but, in his own words:

> The morning of July 24th dawned in a cold drizzle. Arteaga shivered and seemed inclined to stay in his hut. I offered to pay him well if he showed me the ruins. He demurred and said it was too hard a climb for such a wet day. But when he found I was willing to pay him a sol, three or four times the ordinary daily wage, he finally agreed to go. When asked just where the ruins were, he pointed straight up to the top of the mountain. No one supposed that they would be particularly interesting, and no one cared to go with me.

Reading Bingham's words today about this discovery, they seem condescending about Arteaga and at least Eurocentric. Perhaps there is a hint that Bingham fashioned himself after nostalgic perceptions of his hardy New England ancestors who seemed to believe they were innately superior to any natives. Arteaga probably knew best how slippery the nearly vertical climb—about two thousand feet up—would be and how the unmarked trail they would have to create would be crossed by many venomous snakes. After crawling across a rotting rope bridge over the frothing Urubamba, there is no doubt Bingham climbed for hours ever upward through the jungle before finally setting eyes on the astonishing stone masonry ruins of Machu Picchu under a cover of jungle vines atop the ridge. That he was the first English speaker to describe his personal discovery in great detail is probably not debatable. There are other controversies, however, that have surfaced since 1916, in keeping with rising nationalism and debates about cultural patrimony and illicit antiquities.

Controversy over Machu Picchu's collected remains

What happened to the antiquities Hiram Bingham excavated from Machu Picchu's royal tombs and other places at its archaeological site, digging, collecting and cataloging from 1912 to around 1916? Although there has been a battle over the antiquities since the early twentieth century, it has been mostly a private dispute between the Peruvian government and Yale University, which has long claimed the so-called Bingham Collection, as the institutional sponsor of his research at Machu Picchu. Yale has held for decades that Bingham had permission to remove objects—now a debated issue—and to keep a permanent collection at the university after having possibly returned some requested materials.

But times change, as demonstrated by international legal action taken against American museums like the Metropolitan, the Getty and Boston's Museum of Fine Arts, all of which acquired collections of materials in the 1980s and 1990s, materials that Italy, Greece and Turkey, among other countries, claim to have been illicitly excavated and sold illegally without proper documentation or provenance.

In 2001, Alejandro Toledo was duly elected president of Peru, the first indigenous person and Quechua speaker to do so, after generations of Spanish colonialism. Toledo held part of his inauguration at Machu Picchu with somber dignity, a proud reminder of his Inca heritage, which the Spanish-dominated culture had suppressed for centuries. Toledo had started out as a shoeshine boy and eventually won scholarships to schools in the United States, including a degree program in economics at Stanford University. He was heralded for a time as the future of Peru, although the inescapable charges of nepotism so common in Latin America also tainted his administration.

While the issue of repatriating Peruvian material had quietly dragged on for decades between Peru and Yale University, with both sides claiming legal rights of ownership, when Yale staged an exhibition in 2003–5 of some of the contested Machu Picchu material, Peruvians took it very badly. To them it was a diplomatic slap in the face by a global superpower against a developing nation. All hell broke loose.

One article in the *Times* (London) in February 2006 reported:

A battle between Yale University and Peru over treasures from Machu Picchu, the city of the Incas, has highlighted a worrying issue for museum curators: how many prized treasures in their collections are plundered goods that should be restored to the rightful owners? ... The quarrel between Peru and Yale's Peabody Museum is similar, even if Hiram Bingham—the swashbuckling explorer, aviator and professor who discovered Machu Picchu in 1911—won a "special dispensation" from the government to take Inca artefacts out of Peru. For decades, the mainly ceramic treasures sat in boxes at Yale as Peru called for their return. Three years ago, the Peabody staged an Inca exhibition that included artifacts Bingham had brought home. The Peruvians were furious ... Peru threatened to sue Yale and make public its campaign unless the artefacts were returned, but the university insisted it had a proper title to several hundred items and had already returned others.

The diplomatic brouhaha is not yet fully resolved in mid 2006 to the satisfaction of both parties, although Yale has promised to negotiate the return of part of the collection and install them in a museum in Peru. The university will likely keep its word as a demonstration of institutional integrity in the face of world scrutiny, rather than face the charges of vestigial cultural imperialism. Peru, on the other hand, is unwilling to negotiate away its title to the entire collection and lays the onus on Yale for acting in a cavalier way with Peruvian patrimony. Such is the legacy of Machu Picchu that even its remote buried artifacts excavated by an early explorer continue to inspire the imagination and marvel of subsequent generations. Judging by the market in illegal antiquities—not even counting the mostly legal conflict between Peru and Yale—such an Inca or pre-Columbian legacy may also inspire the greed of dealers and collectors.

In 1988 I was with several other archaeologists during an early morning at a Peruvian site, which I will leave unnamed for reasons of safety. One of the first things we noticed when we arrived and were greeted by the site custodians—local Quechuas employed by the Instituto Nacional de Cultura to guard it— were the bulging pockets and dirty hands of these guards, fingernails encrusted with soil. After a short time on-site, certain artifacts, apparently dug up during the night, came out of the guards' pockets and were offered to us for sale. This was not really a surprise, but we had to be careful. We knew if we had bought the objects, the incentive for sales would only stimulate more illegal trafficking and loss to the site, exacerbating the situation.

Such is the huge demand for pre-Columbian artifacts in Europe and North America that what these guards might sell on-site for a few pesos could easily garner hundreds or thousands of dollars in a slick gallery in New York or London. But the outcome is always the same—loss to the archaeological site and the inexorable *caveat emptor*: let the buyer beware. Roger Atwood's recent book, *Stealing History* (2004), lays bare the trail of greed and blood over South American antiquities, among others, that collectors prefer to ignore. The exorbitant prices commanded for them in a European capital city are understandable given the many hands of middlemen through which illicit objects pass, and it should be no surprise that this is accompanied by often sordid stories of organized crime cartels using antiquities for money laundering. Few collectors or dealers of objects acquired after 1970 (when specific international laws were enacted regarding artifacts from some countries fearful of losing their cultural patrimony to outside collectors) can guarantee the provenance of these objects because their methods of acquisition are likely unverifiable. Often legal documents between parties or datable bills for transport of antiquities are missing because they never existed and others were fabricated to fill the gap. The mystique of objects from Inca culture and the very name of Machu Picchu may continue to inspire because the place is so spectacular. In my estimation, Machu Picchu is far more inspiring for those who have walked its terraces than for those who have never seen it firsthand and can only imagine it.

Conclusion: A Personal Machu Picchu

My own experiences in Machu Picchu were not in any way pioneering. The primary research I conducted there was to scientifically confirm the granitoid quarry of the site itself as the immediate "valley" between the Intiwatana and the Great Stairway, and also to augment Inca stoneworking research already begun by Agurto Calvo and Protzen. But my time at Machu Picchu was nonetheless unmistakably part of a personal milestone "high," just as the site has made indelible impressions on everyone who has been there since Hiram Bingham himself.

I remember my own personal discovery of the site of Machu Picchu for the first time after a night slightly downriver, in Aguas Calientes, sleeping in a cot shared with centipedes. The hot springs there—also appreciated by the Inca ruling class—were so blissful that I didn't make much fuss about the critters nestled at the foot of my sleeping bag. The long climb up to Machu Picchu from the Urubamba valley floor must be appreciated firsthand to understand how Hiram Bingham would not have been able to see any ruins from thousands of feet down below, covered as they were by dense high jungle foliage. The towering peaks create a deeply vertical topography that is even more majestic from Machu Picchu itself. At the end of a long day exploring and studying Machu Picchu and conducting stoneworking research, I remember a certain incident as if it happened yesterday, although it was almost two decades ago.

The old Inca rulers had high priest relatives called *amautas* who were an amalgam of amazing skills. They were somehow a combination of poets, composers, astronomers, architects and mathematicians and achieved other intellectual and creative hallmarks in that great culture. *Amautas* not only helped determine the seasons by reckoning with the Intiwatana, the "Hitching Post of the Sun," marking alignment of solstices and other calendrical events to determine when to plant crops, but they also masterminded the rituals of planting and wrote and performed group planting hymns for their people. I happen to love music, and I always carry a recorder flute with me on journeys. While en route

over the Anta highland plateau on our way to the Urubamba valley, we encountered a local festival where all vehicles including
ours were stopped by locals to pay a toll for "*electrificacion*" or
some other purpose. We obliged them with a donation, then we
pulled over, got out of the vehicle and enjoyed the festival. We ate
cuyi asado—roast guinea pig tasting a bit like tangy chicken—
and drank fresh *chicha* corn beer made by toothless Quechua
women spitting corn into a huge vat for quick fermenting. I had
already tried the *chicha frutillada* and the *chicha morada* (fruit and
corn beer) but passed on the *chicha encantada* (the enchanted
hallucinogenic beer).

During this mountain festival, a group of itinerant Quechua
musicians assembled and played armadillo guitars and long
wooden *qena* flutes as well as *zambona* panpipes. Clearly enjoying
themselves, they were both loosely grouped and familiar with the
informal music, taking turns on musical solos. I approached the
band, listening with pleasure and nodding enthusiastically to
the contagious rhythms. Finally with a grin, I took my recorder
flute out of my pocket and waved it shyly at them. Immediately
and without pausing, several Quechua musicians beckoned me
to join them in the music. I was afraid of making a fool of myself
but did not want to be rude or cause insult, so I clambered up on
the crude rickety platform and tried to hide myself—difficult
because I was at least a foot and a half taller—and began quietly
at first to find a common tonal center. I was fairly sure Quechua
music was pentatonic—a scale of five notes like the black keys on
a piano—and this proved true. I found the right pentatonic
"mode" and could play along fairly easily and even found the
syncopated melody delightful. The other players grinned at me,
nodding to the music, and afterward one flautist offered to buy
my flute for what would have been an extravagant sum for him.
I gently shook my head no, and, not wishing to be outdone by

such a display of courtesy, I offered my flute to the man as a gift instead, which I would have regretted had he accepted. To my relief, he didn't accept; it was just an elaborate show of respect. A few days later in Machu Picchu I was grateful I still had my recorder flute because of what happened there.

It was late afternoon at Machu Picchu and my research notebooks were closed and put away in my archaeologist's tough backpack. A light mist was descending through wisps of clouds that hung on the peaks. The site was deserted. I looked for a place to sit and reflect by myself for a few moments. After a few minutes, I found a perfect spot north of the Torreón sun temple. Here I could look out over the deep jungle from a natural amphitheater refashioned into terraces. The jungle disappeared below me into a valley so deep the almost circular fold of the Urubamba River that wrapped around and protected Machu Picchu on three sides could not even be seen. Across the sheer valley, at least a mile distant, cliff walls of granite met the eye. Although I was not sure of it at the time, part of Machu Picchu at this very location has curved descending terraces that create a bowl-like shape, like a megaphone cone enhancing sound qualities—I wondered if its dramatic setting had been intended for performance. I had long studied ancient amphitheaters across many continents, especially Greek and Roman amphitheaters in Europe, the Near East and North Africa. Amazing acoustic qualities are found in nearly every one, a deliberate feature of the ancient architects. Designed echo and reverberation are uncanny in such places. Almost intuitively I pulled out my flute for a few minutes of relaxing play, not really thinking about acoustics, instead being mesmerized by the sheer setting of cliffs looming above and plummeting below. But after playing only a few notes, I was stunned to find an almost perfect echo of my flute melody returning back to me, apparently bouncing off the huge facing vertical granite wall a mile away with only the shortest delay. I could hardly believe it, because there was no decay of sound as one might expect. The echo was almost as loud as the note directly played. The flute notes hung in the air for a few seconds that seemed unreal, apparently also reverberating from the cliffs behind and around me as well.

That began an unforgettable experiment. I thought up a short musical theme, easily remembered, and played it straight toward the far cliff. Pausing, I listened intently and when it returned almost as clear as it went out, I harmonized over it. I almost fell off the amphitheater terrace. It was almost a religious experience, like a miracle. I continued this for some minutes, architecturally adding third and sixth and ninth tones before there was any noticeable decay of sound dimming out in the first and second melody sent out. Even though I had studied and even written about planned acoustics in ancient Greek theaters, I had never heard of anything like this before. It was simply one of the most incredible moments in my life as I continued trying out harmonies and counterpoint melodies for probably close to half an hour. My excitement rose until it was almost unbearable. Near the end, out of the corner of my eye with peripheral vision I finally noticed a few persons had gathered around me, but I was too intent on the sound to even glance over at them. Then something happened that was slightly eerie. The clouds lifted slightly and sun broke through the mist, creating a triple rainbow, the first I had ever witnessed. It was so breathtaking, I used the inspiration to form a musical cadenza climax, gentle but intricate with almost endless arcs of harmonics, at which point I stopped because I was almost frightened by the beauty. As the music finally echoed and reechoed before finally dying away, I sensed there would never be a moment like this again in my life and I shivered.

Then after a minute or two of complete motionless silence, I suddenly realized the small amphitheater was packed with at least twenty people. I looked and saw all the people sitting there were Quechua; I had no idea where they had come from. A man slowly approached me with immense dignity. He looked at me with the most intense but respectful gaze through very thick glass lenses. I rose as he stood before me. He only came up to my chest but had the gravity of a huge man. His words were soft but firm in Quechua-inflected Spanish.

"*Tu es un amauta*. (You are an amauta.)"

"*No, yo no soy un amauta. Solamente un arqueólogo*. (No, I am not an amauta. Only an archaeologist.)"

"No, you are an amauta," he insisted quietly. "*Verdad*. It is true. What you have done here today has not been done for five hundred years. This was a special place for this." His quiet Spanish words were filled with certainty.

I nodded, roughly aware that his people—I later found he was a local headman—were silently observing from a short distance. I wanted to show respect, so I held out my hands and he clasped them in his, never taking his eyes off my face. He spoke again.

"Where did you learn to do this? How did you know?"

I was unsure what he meant. I tried to explain that I didn't know. That I only guessed. How it just seemed perfect when the harmonies were kept alive by echoes. And then the rainbow just happened. But I feel fairly certain he didn't quite believe me. It turned out his people were not officially part of the local Instituto Nacional de Cultura guards who worked around the site of Machu Picchu. I understood they were there guarding its sacredness in their own way, blending into the landscape mostly imperceptibly. I reluctantly left Machu Picchu but I talked to this headman several times and ultimately rode back on the long train trip to Cuzco with him surrounded by his village people as he gently probed me for what else I knew about the Inca. It was difficult in my pidgin Quechua and not-so-fluent Spanish to communicate clearly, but he invited me to visit him near Cuzco in a few days. He wrote his name and address in pencil on a piece of paper, but I was never able to take him up on his offer because I left a few days later.

Since the Quechua headman's first and last words to me were that I was an *amauta*, I had to assume after all that he knew far more about these *amautas* than I did. Understanding more now—but still not enough—about how the *amautas* were the astronomers, architects, artists, poets and composers who led Inca science and art and amazingly integrated both nature and architecture into their mountain landscapes, being called an *amauta* is perhaps the highest compliment I have ever been paid, not just as a professional archaeologist but as one who passionately finds in ancient history the most exciting trail to follow, however far the enticing path leads.

Chapter 6

Pompeii
The Key to Roman Life

Southern Italy, 1748

An Italian farmer, whose name we will probably never know, was digging a well in the rich soil of the sleepy plain under Mount Vesuvius, which often had a column of ashy smoke rising from its dark peak even in 1748. The farmer was trying to reach the sinking water table so his summer crops could flourish. The sound of buzzing cicadas filled the hot air as his oxen stood nearby. His cart was nearly loaded with dirt to the side of a hole he was digging, buried up to his sweaty chest. He continued until he was at least ten feet deep as the soil became more yielding. Suddenly his iron pick hit something harder than the surrounding soil. He stopped and brushed away the dirt. What appeared before his startled eyes was a giant white marble head with staring eyes, looking as if he had just awakened it.

Renewing his digging more carefully, he soon found the head was joined to a colossal statue. It took him most of the day to clear the dirt away and then another hour for his oxen to lift it gingerly into the cart before hauling it to his house nearby.

The next day, the farmer found a trove of other ancient objects and quickly realized he could easily sell his fields for far more than any crops would bring. He contacted the local viceroy, who loved antique art. The news spread like wildfire that a whole city was buried here from almost two thousand years earlier. Soon an unearthed inscription that had been carved on a now-broken portal even told the forgotten name of the lost city: Pompeii. . . . This story is so difficult to confirm that we can only wonder what the farmer's name was or if it's even true.

Few in 1748 would have guessed the fate that had quickly over-taken Pompeii. Even fewer would fathom at the time that its dis-covery would forever change what we know about Roman material culture, far more than any other single site. The enor-mous significance of its long-buried artifacts nearly outweighs all the remaining bulk of Roman artifacts put together. Many good reasons exist why Pompeii should be on any list of the most important discoveries in history, but here are a few primary ones. The catastrophe of Vesuvius buried Pompeii in little more than forty-eight hours, and we have eyewitness accounts written at the time. This accidental discovery of Pompeii in 1748 happened before archaeology was a science, and Pompeii became a magnet for travelers and collectors from the 1750s onward. Following its discovery, eighteenth- and nineteenth-century literature about Pompeii made its forgotten tragedy famous to an eager audience. Furthermore, the modern impact of continuing archaeological work at Pompeii has continued its original legacy. Surviving Pom-peiian buildings help define Roman architecture, and Pompeii's collections represent the best examples of Roman art. (Although Herculaneum was likely discovered first, with cursory excavation beginning around 1735, it was covered much deeper than Pom-peii, with harder solidified mudstone and lava, and was therefore abandoned for decades more. As of this writing, Pompeii is still

only around 65 percent excavated based on what remains unex-
plored inside the Roman city walls.)

The ensuing legacy of Pompeii's past catastrophe and present
blessing can hardly be appreciated. What is known about everyday Roman life is immeasurably determined by what has been
unearthed at Pompeii since that farmer dug his well. Here is a
salient fact: virtually 25 percent of what the world has collected
from Roman material culture comes from being preserved by
this one brief volcanic eruption that sealed an entire city, preserving much of its life even in death.

The buried city of Pompeii in its dying days of August AD 79
could never have known that its great misfortune would eventually grab the attention of the world. By the sheer volume of artifacts found there alone, no other site has provided so much
knowledge about ancient Roman life. Because of the quickness of
the catastrophe and the haste of the abandonment, no other place
on earth has yielded such vast material documenting daily affairs
and everyday possessions. The artifacts range from ivory combs
to wall paintings, from scorched and carbonized papyri to gems
and house pets, from priceless treasures in cameo glass to priceless records of the mundane including daily diet. Loaves of
carbonized bread still on the table or in the ovens of ruined
households, burned walnuts and even garden roots have been
preserved. It has taken centuries to begin to assess the wealth of
scholarship from Pompeii, and it is far from complete. But we
can reconstruct much of the disastrous event in the summer of
AD 79 as well as how Pompeiians lived up until that very day.

August 24, AD 79

On August 24 in AD 79, the long but late hot summer of
southern Italy would have shown the typical heat waves shim-

mering off the circling mountains and the dramatic blue water of the Bay of Naples. Before the heat of the day, the early morning streets would have been filled as usual with shoppers going to and from open-air markets and citizens scurrying about in the shade whenever possible. Down at the wharf, fish of all kinds were sold directly from the dawn's catches off Cape Misenum, where the water teemed with life. Vegetables and fruit were abundant in the Campanian soil. More than one poet or writer wrote truthfully about this place being Campania Felix, "Happy Campania." Pliny the Elder, who died in the eruption, wrote in his encyclopedic *Natural History* before AD 79: "There is one region where Nature has been at work in her joyous mood: Campania, the climate so temperate, the plains so fertile, the hills so sunny, the groves so shady." Ironically, the city had just celebrated its Volcanalia festivities to the god Vulcan, the patron of craftsmen, famous for his divinely hot smithy where the god was said to forge and hammer molten iron from underneath the surrounding mountains.

If the citizens of Pompeii ever looked carefully down at their sandaled feet while they stepped across the paving, they might have noticed all of the dark paving stones, many naturally shaped in hexagons, were of solidified lava from nearby volcanic sources. The whole region was volcanic, a land where the magmatic lava had cooled and crystallized, eventually to be revealed at the surface and extracted from quarries. After eons of rain, sun, wind and other natural forces, much of the lava had broken down into soil. The fields around Pompeii were the richest and most fertile in Italy from the uncounted and mostly forgotten millennia of sporadic eruptions rich in ash and minerals. If they had looked up and seen Mount Vesuvius brooding over them, it was normal in the region of Campania for people to seek its cooler slopes for its sweeping vistas of the sparkling bay below and even plant lush vineyards climbing the peak. Very few must have recognized or wondered about the danger in store.

These Pompeiians were blessed, as everyone knew, since Pompeii was also the richest Roman port for luxury goods from Egypt and the East. Ships constantly sailed in and out of the harbor at the mouth of the Sarno River. Its dockside warehouses were filled with exotic goods to be dispersed to the wealthy throughout Italy and the rest of the empire, including the most precious commodities like frankincense, silk and pearls. The Bay of Naples, with its smaller towns of Herculaneum, Oplontis and Stabiae, was highly sought after for palatial residences away from Rome, and the Pompeiians' huge coastal villas were laden with bronze and marble sculptures and lovely gardens. This was a veritable paradise where senatorial patrician families could relax near vast farms tended by numerous tenants and slaves and where local produce was crisp and cool because it had just been plucked or cut a few minutes earlier from the fragrant soil. Flowers bloomed everywhere on trellises and on the ground around low ornamental boxwood hedges. Judging by the opulent art of Pompeii, food was as plentiful on land as in the sea. In Pompeiian paintings, luscious fruits hang pendulous on trees; multitudes of fish gape from intricate Pompeiian mosaic floors whose tiny tiles are less than a quarter inch across. If the excavated art masterpieces are any index, clearly there were fortunes to be spent and made in wealthy Pompeii.

This was a city lucky in love too, as one of its patron goddesses was Venus herself, the icon of physical love, who blessed this people with deep passion and either a rich love life or the powerful fantasy of one. Her temple crowned the height of the city above the Sarno River and her presence was evident in vivid reminders all over the city: famous *lupenare* brothels on the heavily trafficked corners, innumerable phallic images stamped in brick or carved on walls, and painted or inscribed advertisements of exotic prostitutes whose names scrawled in civic graffiti claimed they could satisfy every physical craving. If anything typified the city of Pompeii in AD 79, it was prosperity, luxury and excess in nature as in human appetites. Who could find a better life anywhere in the Roman world than here under the shadow of Vesuvius?

The catastrophe of Vesuvius buried Pompeii in little more than forty-eight hours

August twenty-fourth must have dawned like every other summer morning in memory. But suddenly in a few hours everything changed. It is not difficult to reconstruct the events based on archaeology, volcanology and eyewitness accounts. Pompeii's citizens had long tolerated the frequent tremors that shook the ground as a fair price to pay for living in the most beautiful region of Italy. But the early afternoon quiet of August 24 was broken by an explosion that jolted the whole city awake from its after-lunch nap. A sound louder than anything imaginable blasted the trembling air and buildings rocked on their foundations. Dust and chips fell everywhere as people ran in panic out into the streets to see what was happening. The sun must have been quickly blotted out by dark billowing clouds of ash and lapilli—tiny stones from the size of hail to golf balls—often of light pumice but also of heavier volcanic ejecta that would have begun falling quickly into the streets and pelting the roofs with incessant drumming. Although they would not have realized it, the entire top of the mountain had been blown apart and sent into the air, its force impelling everything up against gravity, sending millions of tons of rock, ash, steam and smoke along with poisonous gases higher than the clouds. Thousands of feet up in the air, the debris formed into a column that spread out like a giant tree with ominous branches visible for scores of miles as it descended, only to be replaced by more. Immediately around Pompeii and the surrounding towns, the midday became as dark as night. Handheld clay lamps would hardly have penetrated the gloom of dense ash falling everywhere and quickly piling up several feet deep in a matter of an hour or so.

Most of the approximately twenty-five thousand residents of Pompeii must have fled fairly quickly but many also stayed behind, either out of fear, hiding in the crowded alleys under eaves or inside buildings themselves, thinking it was safer, or because they might have thought it an opportune moment to rob with impunity a quickly emptying city. The authorities must not have known what to do other than flee themselves through the rubble and rain of stones. The proud city became total chaos. The sensible ones would have left quickly, abandoning almost all of their belongings, thinking only of saving their lives and those of their loved ones. Others would have quickly locked houses or gates and sought the safest exit to the countryside or the harbor.

But few knew that the harbor and the river itself were being blocked by either the geological effects of uplift or a receding coastline combined with a dammed river, and they were stranded on rocky dry ground at the wharves. Boats were empty without water for escape. Hundreds of people, including whole families, huddled in the dockside warehouses under or alongside useless boats. Here dense gases quickly settled with their poisonous stench, and the superheated air was actually burning in places. Anoxia quickly overcame people; they were already being choked by ash falling so thickly that they were asphyxiated by a number of deadly elements. A gaseous surge of boiling liquid ash swept through the burning city in the night and ended many lives of the trapped or hiding citizens who had survived the first hours. Many families must have been separated and many indistinguishable crying voices must have been heard everywhere. Husbands and wives, choking and holding futile cloths against their noses and mouths to breathe, were lying together with their children clutched against them to take their last embraces as a thick quiet descended, punctuated only by the almost silent fall of ash and the intermittent rain of small and large stones against groaning roofs. The whole city was buried in an afternoon and a night of mostly volcanic ash mixed with lapilli and pumice that piled up more than twenty-five feet deep in places. In other places it piled even higher, so that it was above the rooftops of two-story buildings. An estimated 2,500 Pompeiians perished that day, although we may never know the exact total loss of life. This was truly the day a city died. Yet, without denying the tragedy of its citizens in this sudden destruction, important to archaeology and history is the fact that the sudden event of this volcanic eruption sealed much of the city of Pompeii from normal decay.

Eyewitness accounts were written at the time

The careful records of shocked but literate Romans who were eyewitnesses to the cataclysm were not lost, but rather merely ignored and then forgotten in ensuing centuries. Pliny the Younger, writing almost immediately after Pompeii's destruction to his friend, the eminent historian Tacitus, about his uncle Pliny the Elder's death, said this about the panic-stricken city:

For several days before there had been earth tremors which were not particularly alarming because they are frequent in Campania, but that night the shocks were so violent that everything felt as if it were not only shaken but overturned . . . You could hear the shrieks of women, the wailing of infants, and the shouting of men; some were calling their parents, others their children or their wives, trying to recognize them by their voices. People bewailed their own fate or that of their relatives, and there were some who prayed for death in their terror of dying. Many besought the aid of the gods, many more imagined there were no gods left and that the universe was plunged into eternal darkness for evermore.

For another whole day and a half, the eruption of Vesuvius buried not only Pompeii but the town of Herculaneum, as well as sumptuous villas on the harbor at Oplontis and Stabiae and nearby at Greco del Torre, Boscoreale and Boscotrecase. Three days later the eruption had finally all but subsided, the sea breeze returned and the summer sun shone dimly through the smoke of still-burning houses. But the lovely verdant landscape of the plain sloping to the sea was forever changed. Survivors who had fled returned in small numbers, perhaps to see how total the ruin was or to retrieve what they could; strangers also came from several days' journey away to see for themselves what had happened, but all were unnerved by the total devastation. The fertile plain was reduced to the aftermath of an inferno.

Within seventy-two hours of the eruption, word quickly reached Rome by hurried messengers of the official *cursus publicus*, the official Roman courier network, or by military dispatch from the navy at Misenum. Immediately the new emperor himself, Titus, came down to Campania with an entourage of soldiers and officials to see the smoking devastation and the blank countryside, once green and leafy, now brown and empty. After hearing reports of people—mostly survivors seeking relatives or lost goods—who had inadvertently fallen through the smoldering debris of sagging roofs everywhere and were burned alive in hot ash, the emperor declared the whole region unsafe and that it was to be completely abandoned, and his imperial decree was published on penalty of death for disobedience. Thus Pompeii was left alone as the ash settled and hardened. And the memory was recalled only with a silent shudder.

What happened to Pompeii after its sudden burial is perhaps not so dramatic until more than a millennium and a half later. Although the plain was gradually resettled long after Emperor Titus's edict, aided by fast-growing vegetation in the greatly enriched volcanic ash topsoil, it wasn't until the eighteenth century, in a completely different world, that Pompeii was rediscovered. By then nobody paid much attention to the occasional buried remains coming to light from the entombed city below that had been more populous than the rural surface. One might ask why it took so long, but the truth is rather simple. First, the Roman ruling culture and Titus's strict law lasted for almost five hundred years, by which time the diminished remnants of Roman Italy had completely forgotten what had happened. Those who knew what was entombed became gradually fewer; those who could read Pliny fewer still. Second, the Romans were a superstitious and religious people who revered their ancestors and would not have dared to disturb the mass entombment for fear of divine reprisals worse than any imperial edict. Furthermore, perhaps many Pompeiians who survived the volcanic conflagration would not have remained in the immediate area out of fear or a healthy respect for what volatile nature had done. After a few generations, after being warned to stay away from a place cursed by the gods or nature, Pompeii was forgotten.

Initial excavation of Pompeii happened for art, not science

According to history, Pompeii was discovered by an Italian farmer, as noted at the beginning of this chapter, then was exploited by a Spanish king, promoted by a British cuckold, written about early on by a German who would be brutally murdered in notoriety, and then later excavated under a Fascist dictator.

The Spanish king ruling over Naples in 1748 was the Bourbon king Charles III, who sent many priceless Pompeiian sculptures to Spain. The British cuckold was the diplomat Sir William Hamilton, who helped put Pompeii on the antiquities map for collectors and on the Grand Tour, and whose wife, Emma, had an infamous affair with Lord Nelson, vaunted admiral of the Napoleonic era. The German scholar who published Pompeiian art was Johann Joachim Winckelmann, the "Father of Classical Archaeology," but his brilliant career ended when he was murdered in an inn by one of his male lovers in a secret tryst gone bad. The great Italian archaeologist Amedeo Maiuri in the 1930s was not necessarily happy that his boss was Il Duce, the demagogue dictator Mussolini who wanted to revive Rome's glory, but Maiuri achieved remarkable results excavating at Pompeii, and those who followed him have hailed from many countries, since Pompeii is seen to belong not just to Italy but to the world.

The initial story of the anonymous Italian farmer accidentally discovering Pompeii in 1748 while digging a well may only be anecdotal because his name is not recorded or verifiable. Pompeii's rediscovery may not have been as dramatic as its destruction, but it is certainly a vital historic saga by itself. The first glimmers of what antiquities lay under the surface of the Campanian region came about under foreign domination, as Spain ruled the Kingdom of the Two Sicilies from the capital of Naples. To the immediate north of the Bay of Naples were the Phlegrean Fields, the infamous "Fields of Fire," land of sulfuric smoking fumaroles and mythical world of the Cumaean Sibyl, an oracle indigenous to Italy whom Michelangelo had painted on the Sistine Chapel. As early as 1613, some artifacts of the AD 79 Vesuvian destruction of the Campanian region began to surface, but it would be years before these sporadic discoveries were connected to the same event.

In 1734, the Spanish Bourbon Charles III came to the throne in Naples, quickly following his mother's Farnese family instincts for collecting antiquities. In 1748 excavations seeking buried sculpture began at Pompeii, probably on the heels of similar reports like the farmer digging a well. The news eventually came to the ears of the king himself. King Charles appointed Rocco Gioacchino de Alcubierre, a Spanish survey engineer, to dig up and supply the court with ancient statuary extracted from the plain in known rich sites. The engineer dug up material from a spot in Pompeii close to the Temple of Fortuna Augusta, but soon moved his efforts to Herculaneum because it was perceived as having more buried treasure. A year later in Gragnano, the king's workers began to exploit the buried town of Stabiae along the bay. Pompeii itself was excavated again in 1754 and in 1763. The inscription with the name of Pompeii finally located the city of Pliny's description. Unearthing the name was such a significant event that the great engraver and restorer Giovanni Battista Piranesi records the rediscovered name Pompeii in his dramatic art.

Pompeii was a magnet for travelers from the 1750s onward

As its buried structures began to yield enormous numbers of artifacts, Pompeii soon became the most important stop on the Grand Tour of Europe by the nobility and other wealthy collectors; thus Pompeii became a magnet for travelers. Many would make special trips to Italy on the reputation of Pompeii alone and Europeans from Paris, London, Berlin, Copenhagen, St. Petersburg and many other cities all made Naples and Pompeii necessary stops on their travel itineraries.

The findings were so rich, with scores of separate supervised teams soon digging all over the Pompeiian landscape, that the Spanish king was careful to control everything personally, setting up royal franchises for archaeological excavations on a scale never before seen. The importance of these artifacts was not seen at first, when the royal agenda was originally planned just for sculpture and monuments. But then whole buildings began to appear skeletally, one by one, from under the soft tufa at Pompeii. *Tufa* is a generic geological term for old volcanic ash consolidated to a rock not much harder than chalk in many places. Reports spread quickly to Rome and then beyond Italy along eighteenth-century channels via correspondence and diplomatic pouch as well as word of mouth. The whole of educated Europe with its proud universities soon woke up to a world lost for almost two millennia. The Grand Tour was born, a travel itinerary leading from Rome and various ancient Italian sites to Naples in order to view these new proceedings with wonder. Never before had an ancient buried city been discovered so complete, down to table settings and bedposts. Add to that volume the desirable treasures of sardonyx, carnelian and agate gems and gold jewelry as well as bronze vessels, silver tableware, Roman glass and even carbonized furniture. Pompeii had an almost uncountable abundance of everyday household items and precious objects, many of which, because they have not survived elsewhere, had never been seen before.

To nearly all visitors, the manner of Pompeii's demise was itself fairly easy to understand and became an obvious attraction of modern sympathy to ancient tragedy. That thousands died was perhaps less interesting than the fact that people could ascertain the exact moment and manner of death. This alone was a powerful and fascinating draw.

Many artists came to draw and paint the romantic ruins, and scholars came alongside collectors to learn all they could. One of the most remarkable novelties in the eyes of the scholars was the prolific Roman wall paintings that were virtually unknown before Pompeii, as the city of Rome had hardly any surviving Roman painting intact.

In 1750 the king adapted the Bourbon royal villa at nearby Portici to temporarily house the staggering collection of artifacts that was growing daily; it became a "Museo Herculanense." The famous Oplontis villa of Julius Caesar's father-in-law, Cornelius Piso, soon supplied a whole library of carbonized papyrus scrolls in the years 1754–58 as literal caverns were dug under that seaside town. The king indirectly chartered the Accademia Ercolanese to begin publishing the royal collections in 1755. The royal excavations at Pompeii and the vicinity required a bureaucracy of civil servants to record and document the thousands of objects, let alone house and curate them.

Charles, in the remarkable spirit of an innovating monarch who had no precedent to follow, allowed his administration to initiate a formal scientific establishment at Pompeii. Part of Charles's staff was overseen by local scholars from the venerable University of Naples, or antiquarians like Camillo Paderni from Rome, in charge of the Museo Herculanense, and the French sculptor Joseph Canart, who supervised sculptural restoration. One of the king's able noble ministers and a trusted friend was the Marquis Bernardo Tanucci, himself an antiquarian collector/scholar from Tuscany, and some of his official duties extended to supervision of the Pompeii excavations for the king. The king was fortunate to have these and other cognizant officials who made initial decisions that would set the stage for generations of future archaeologists. It was not until much later, in 1860, that an astute archaeologist named Giuseppe Fiorelli saw the tufa cavities and lacunae themselves as potential artifacts: by pouring plaster of paris into the cavities, human effigies soon emerged in the very contortions of death by asphyxiation. One fact was plain: Rome had nothing compared to the plain of Naples. Buildings like the Pantheon that had survived on Rome's surface were few and far between. Here was a whole plain of intact ghostly cities quickly coming to light.

On the other hand, in the early "Neapolitan approach" of the eighteenth century, practicality was the guiding force behind pioneering conservation experiments. Such methods included brushing a protective application of melted wax varnish over plastered surfaces. This did much to preserve hundreds of the wall paintings that had been hidden from light so long, whereas paintings left alone on the walls at Pompeii soon oxidized in the pigment-fading photolysis of the hot Neapolitan sunlight.

Some of the early travelers drawn to Pompeii's growing fame were legends in their own right. Johann Wolfgang von Goethe, Germany's greatest Romantic genius and author of *Faust*, came to Italy in 1786–87. Goethe's portrait in Campania, painted by Johann Tischbein, shows Goethe informally sprawled in travel garb over the ruined landscape in cape and hat, surrounded by sculpture. In his *Italian Journey* from that year Goethe left his singular impressions of Pompeii, as well as keen observations; for example, describing the Villa of Diomedes in some detail, he writes:

Pompeii surprises all by its dense compactness . . . with narrow straight streets and sidewalks . . . small houses without windows . . . but imaginatively and colorfully decorated and painted . . . Although the city, having first been buried under a rain of ash and stone and then looted by its excavators, is completely destroyed by now, it still witnesses artistic instinct and love of art . . . To picture more clearly what happened historically, one should imagine a mountain village buried by snow.

Literature on Pompeii made its forgotten tragedy famous to an eager audience

Pompeii was a magnet to a world that tried to imagine the lost city's final hours, much as Edward Bulwer-Lytton attempted in 1834 with his florid novel *The Last Days of Pompeii*. Another early British antiquarian and scholar at Pompeii was Sir William Gell, writing his *Pompeiana* in 1817 after years in the area. Literary descriptions of Pompeii run the gamut from romantically poetic to pedantic. René de Chateaubriand visited in 1804 and published his *Voyage en Italie* in 1824. It should not be a surprise that the Marquis de Sade, ever the explorer and observer of pain, visited and wrote a bit about Pompeii in 1775 in his *Voyage d'Italie*. Literati who visited and unforgettably described Pompeii include the poet Théophile Gautier, who wrote a tale about a tragic young Pompeiian girl in his *Arria Marcella* in 1852. Alexandre Dumas— also appointed by Garibaldi for a short time as director of the Museo Nazionale at Naples—wrote *Le Corricolo* about Pompeii in 1843.

Pompeii also was more influential than any other ancient site in forming the Grand Tour across the Mediterranean. It was the de rigueur stop for the noble and upper middle classes in search of antiquity as a component of education. Virtually every head of state and member of European royalty had to come to view Pompeii, where "new discoveries" were staged for their benefit. Naturally, among the countless visitors to Pompeii in the nineteenth century was the widely traveled Charles Dickens, who in his *Pictures from Italy* in 1846 described Pompeii thus:

Look up the silent streets . . . over the broken houses . . . to Mt. Vesuvius . . . in the strange and melancholy sensation of seeing the Destroyed and the Destroyer making this quiet picture. Then ramble on, and see at every turn the familiar tokens of human habitation and every-day pursuits . . . the track of carriage wheels in the pavement of the street; the marks of drinking vessels on the stone counter of the wine shop; the amphorae in private cellars, stored away so many hundred years ago, and undisturbed to this hour—all rendering the solitude and deadly lonesomeness of the place, ten thousand times more solemn, than if the volcano in its fury had swept the city from the earth and sunk it in the bottom of the sea . . . We watch Vesuvius as it disappears from the prospect, and watch for it again on our return, with the same thrill of interest: as the doom and destiny of all this beautiful country, biding its terrible time.

The modern impact of Pompeii has continued its archaeological legacy

Pompeii would become an arbiter of archaeological field methods for centuries, each generation building on the experience as well as mistakes of prior excavations. Having been appointed by King Victor Emmanuel II in 1860, the same able archaeologist

Giuseppe Fiorelli who had pioneered the plaster of paris casting of the victims also published three volumes of his comprehensive tome *Pompeianarum Antiquitatem Historia*. His "History of Antiquities of the Pompeiians," written and made available between 1860 and 1864, is an immensely quantitative record of finds, many merely ordinary, some quite gruesome. Thanks to Fiorelli, there are scores of plaster casts of victims spread throughout Pompeii in their death poses. One of the most poignant is the cast of a small child found under the stairs in the House of the Golden Bucket. He (or she) was perhaps three or four years old and facial features (including shut eyelids) are nearly perfectly preserved at the moment of a sleeplike death. In the dockside warehouses parents have locked arms lovingly over a child they could not protect from this calamity. In the House of Julius Polybius, among twelve other victims, a young pregnant teenager was found clutching her hastily gathered belongings to her chest with a few gold and silver coins. Others died not so peacefully as we would like to imagine, like the dog writhing on its back as it chokes on the ash and burning air, its gasping mouth wide open. Based on excavations from the nineteenth century onward, especially under Giuseppe Fiorelli, Pompeii is divided today into nine districts, somewhat in chronological sequence of their excavation histories.

Because Pompeii has always been at the forefront of archaeological research, it is still a place where experimental techniques were pioneered that were then followed elsewhere. The twentieth century saw renewed archaeological excavations of a more modern nature, ambitiously unearthing new sectors previously covered. Under an organized Soprintendenza, the official bureaucracy overseeing cultural property, Pompeii came of age as the world's grande dame of vintage archaeology and the fashionable focus of modern scholarship. The great "Prince among Archaeologists," Amedeo Maiuri, took advantage in the 1930s of Mussolini's intention to recast the new Italian state as a continuation of the old Roman one that had controlled the world by inspiring authority. Pompeii was an opportunity to showcase Roman urbanism, so huge tracts of new excavations laid bare larger parts of the buried city. According to Robert Etienne in *Pompeii: The Day a City Died* (1992), Maiuri defined what is presently seen of Pompeii by his extensive excavations. At the end of the twentieth century, Antonio Varone continued excavating Pompeii but without the propagandizing vision of Fascism. International efforts also encouraged collaborative projects between nations and academic institutions to keep Pompeii at the cutting edge of archaeology, which is only fitting for the world's most famous archaeological site.

Unfortunately, on the other hand, protecting what has been long unearthed has not always been as important. Conservation of buildings and objects on the vast site has often not kept pace with current unearthing of the Roman city, and Pompeii is badly in need of repairs. Rampant vandalism has destroyed many clay amphorae that used to grace buildings. Repair work is a constant need as reconstructed timbers rot and the hordes of visitors take their toll on the old buried city, a city that was in better shape when not exposed to the elements. Between the effects of humidity and winter rainfall, archaeological tourism, and lack of conservation, the site that became the blueprint for archaeology may become precarious, its very continuity and survival threatened.

Visitors from abroad simply must see Pompeii if they are within a hundred miles of Naples, if they truly want to be educated about Roman life. Pompeii is an education in itself and it is unfathomable not to see it if able. "Pompeii is a household name," says Andrew Wallace-Hadrill, director of the British School in Rome.

More people visit Pompeii now in one single day than in whole seasons of the previous centuries. Pompeii often sees more than fifty-five thousand visitors a day in midsummer. It is still the most visited intact ancient city in Europe. Strangely, despite the masses of tourists, one can still be the solo visitor on a lonely street corner in Pompeii where the only faces seen are those carved on stone fountains at road junctions. Anyone from the last century who has spent much time in Pompeii, walking its paved streets or peering into its ghostly houses, or in the treasure house where its artifacts are stored, the great National Museum in Naples, invariably encounters this fact: even with myriad inventories that can hardly be counted from over two hundred years of excavation, the mind-boggling reality is that this massive collection covers barely two days of destruction.

Pompeiian structures help define Roman architecture

One of the most important facts to understand about Pompeii is how much its preserved urban skeleton has helped historians and archaeologists reconstruct the general architectural plan of a Roman city, an urban planning pattern repeated wherever the Romans went. These features common to any Roman city are abundantly clear at Pompeii. The Romans usually built new cities around a forum, the administrative, religious, commercial and judicial core, with temples, courts, markets and the like. Pompeii is filled with the clearest examples of these urban units, up to three and four yards high, where most ruined Roman cities have only remnant foundations left, barely a few feet high.

In the overall Roman urban plan, two major thoroughfares provide the directional axes of a city, the north-south *cardo maximus* and the east-west *decumanus maximus*, often leading to major city gates wherever possible. If the city began from a fortified military encampment called a *castra*, the resulting square-shaped city may be surrounded by a wall. Minor streets branch off from the two main avenues. Distributed along these two axes were theaters, amphitheaters, public and private baths and other civic structures as well as residences. Our word *domicile* derives from the Roman word *domus*, a large urban residential house.

Thanks to Pompeii, we know a typical Roman house is essentially a walled courtyard with an entrance but without windows. The grander Roman houses multiply elements such as interior courtyards (colonnaded peristyles) around other rooms or features. Pompeiian houses rarely deviate from this idea, also following a common pattern with at least one street side entrance into an atrium, a small colonnaded courtyard with a rainwater catchment basin called an *impluvium* (roughly meaning "rainwater [goes] into [it]"). Beyond this the house pattern may follow the inner peristyle, garden (*hortus*) and wings (*alae*) of the house with a three-couch-studded dining room (*triclinium*) and a highly decorated formal reception room (*tablinum*). It is possible in some houses that one can see all the way through the house from atrium to peristyle, and beyond to the kitchen (*culina*) and bedrooms (*cubiculae*), as well as to an outer courtyard. In most houses, a private *lararium* contained the house shrines kept to revere ancestors.

Pompeii has most likely added more to the historical perception of the typical Roman house than any other site. Nearby Herculaneum is more of a town than a city like Pompeii and its houses were usually larger, but it is Pompeii that best represents a Roman city for understanding urban Roman life.

Pompeii's collections represent the best examples of Roman art

Pompeii was certainly a morbid fascination for some, but it was even more appreciated by savants and art collectors or antiquarians like Sir William Hamilton. Securing a diplomatic post as the British minister plenipotentiary, Hamilton became known as the "Volcano Lover." He arrived in Naples in 1764 and ultimately climbed Vesuvius a score of times even during the frequent new eruptions of Vesuvius of the late eighteenth century. Although he was well known in his day as both a diplomat and a collector, he was also a cuckold, the tolerant husband of the infamously beautiful Lady Emma Hamilton, who became Lord Nelson's lover. Hamilton's 1775 portrait by David Allan from the collection of the National Portrait Gallery in London (now on permanent loan to the British Museum) shows a slender, hawk-nosed aging aristocrat of dignity standing in his crimson Knight of the Order of the Bath regalia next to a window through which Vesuvius is seen smoking in the distant sunset. Along with the efforts of the Society of the Dilettanti, a mostly aristocratic group of young British aesthetes who appreciated ancient art, Hamilton's collection helped form the inspiration and backbone of the early British Museum collections of Roman art. Much of Hamilton's Roman art collection was obtained in Naples and from Pompeiian contexts.

Roman wall painting would be virtually nonexistent without Pompeii. Only a few handfuls of extant paintings elsewhere can even begin to compare to the hundreds found at Pompeii. Most of these were cleverly transported to the National Museum in Naples but many can still be seen on-site. They are of such a quantity, so definitive and so well preserved, that for at least a century now, Roman art historians have divided the spectacular wall paintings of Pompeii into four datable phases between the second century BC to AD 79 when Pompeii was snuffed out. Although many Pompeiian wall paintings are architectural or dramatic fantasies, they show that remarkable realism was a Roman accomplishment long before the Renaissance. Treasures like the Wounded Aeneas, Europa Riding a Bull, and Bacchus painted as a grape cluster before an unerupted Vesuvius are gems. To best understand the importance of Pompeii and its art, both the ruined city and the National Museum in Naples must be seen together.

Roman mosaics are also wonderfully preserved from Pompeii, many of them listed as the most important in the world, such as the Battle of Issus mosaic depicting Alexander the Great meeting King Darius of Persia in 333 BC. This mosaic dates to about 100 BC, and it is made up of at least a million small tessera tiles, most of which are smaller than a quarter inch across. It is massive, around seventeen by nine feet, and its incredible range of warm colors is subtle, with many hues of brown and creamy tones even in its incomplete remnants. Discovered in 1831 in the House of the Faun, Goethe remarked about it the following year:

Neither the present nor the future will be able to comment fittingly on such a remarkable work of art, and we shall be eternally obliged, after all our studies and explanations, to contemplate it in wonder pure and simple.

Other famous Pompeiian mosaics include a Sea Scene Fish Market that is remarkably lifelike—so realistic that the almost three-dimensional fish and other sea life still have gaping mouths and bulging eyes that look freshly wet. Marine biologists can still identify every species here from the Bay of Naples because each is rendered so perfectly, whether octopus, lobster, squid, red mullet, moray eel, skate or murex. Also famous is the *Cave canem*— "Beware of Dog"—mosaic that can be seen on the site in a forlorn doorway, still guarding the house as a reminder of a once-living dog that it resembles. These examples represent only a selected microcosm of Pompeii's art.

Bronze and marble sculptures, famous cameo treasures of thinly carved sardonyx agate stone, and many other treasures came from Pompeii, giving us the most complete picture we have about Roman art. One can hardly open a text on Roman art without noting that the majority of examples derive from Pompeii and its neighboring towns.

There is no way to do justice in one brief chapter to the literally tens of thousands of objects of art and craft or the huge quantity of utilitarian household goods from Pompeii, but the city of Pompeii needs to be seen in tandem with the National Museum in Naples to give an idea of the quantity and quality of materials excavated in two and half centuries. No other museum in the world is devoted to primarily one event, with so many masterpieces and defining archetypes of human activity and art all derived from a few square miles in a several-day cataclysm.

Conclusion

In retrospect, it is the eyewitness Pliny the Younger in AD 79 whom modern volcanologists credit with first describing in his letters what is now called a "Plinian" eruption. Trained by his uncle and namesake to observe everything carefully, Pliny was amazingly accurate in geological detail, from rains of pumice and lapilli to pyroclastic flow and atmospheric disturbances. We now know the Plinian eruption at Vesuvius was due to several factors of deep internal geomorphology. Below the Bay of Naples, seawater and groundwater seeped ever downward through cracks in the crustal earth toward high-temperature magma in an active volcanic zone below Vesuvius, ultimately forming a body of water in occasional contact with vents and cracks where magma surged upward. Trapped water such as this boils and creates tremendous steam pressure that can explode whole mountains of rock in a pyrotechnic display rarely seen. This also caused the eruption of Krakatoa in 1883, the "shot heard round the world" where a whole island disappeared in a matter of minutes.

At the end of the nineteenth century, the philosopher Nietzsche satirically commented about modern life in general, "Go ahead, build your house on Mt. Vesuvius." Anyone driving by Vesuvius today will see just that: modern houses are again creeping up the slopes even though the local provincial government has offered relocation money to offset the ignored peril. It's true, the views are fantastic, and real estate on Mount Vesuvius is a relative bargain considering the risk, but no smart insurers will offer policies. The last eruption was in 1944. How many Neapolitans can even remember its billowing column of smoke captured on dramatic black-and-white photos at the time? These photos are older than all the lively young Neapolitans who career around on buzzing Vespas, sometimes four to a scooter, through the infamously wild traffic where horns and brakes interchange in cacophony. One cannot help but notice how similar humans are to our antecedents. The beauty of Naples is justifiably mirrored in its handsome citizens, who resemble their Greek and Roman ancestors in their capricious love of life. Their ability to laugh at destiny does not mock history but allows them a fatalistic appreciation of the moment and of ephemera, enjoying short life to the hilt. Neapolitans today know that Campania Felix is no myth even in the shadow of Vesuvius. A famous phrase still rings across Europe. In musical Italian it sings bittersweetly: *Vedi Napoli e poi muori*. "See Naples and then die." Like Pompeii before it, Naples is still so full of reckless life.

Perhaps the Pompeiians should have heeded the warning from a massive earthquake that shook the city so badly in AD 63 that repairs were still being made when Vesuvius finally blew sixteen years later. Perhaps slightly contemporary Roman geographers like Strabo (who died circa AD 24), who had observed active vulcanism at Mount Etna in Sicily, may have noticed the volcanic cone similarity in Vesuvius. Perhaps he should have left some public records for future Romans as warnings against the potential devastation, since villages were regularly evacuated in the path of Etna's spewing molten streams of fire. But whatever hindsight is applicable, one thing is certain: Pompeii's great misfortune is our fortune. Endless artifacts fill almost an entire national museum, and libraries will never exhaust the continuing study of Pompeii.

So unlike typical archaeological material—usually broken and fragmentary—from most sites, Pompeii's artifacts and those of the surrounding towns are remarkably intact and complete. A whole nomenclature of archaeology was invented and applied to deal with Pompeii's discovery and subsequent revelation to a world curious and itself deeply sympathetic to the shuddering of a lost city. Pompeii not only opened up a lost world, its discovery fueled a new discipline. Thus, modern archaeology can be traced back to the discovery of Pompeii.

If a citizen of Pompeii from before AD 79 were to be suddenly thrust into the Pompeii, or neighboring town of Herculaneum, of today, the city is so intact that this person could return to his or her house on its street and usually find it quite easily. This is unlike any other ancient place in the Roman world, and that is one reason why many archaeologists believe Pompeii is now probably more important to archaeology than the great imperial city of Rome itself.

Chapter 7

Dead Sea Scrolls
The Key to Biblical Research

Dead Sea cliffs, 1947

Two boys in the Judean desert in 1947 made what is probably the most important biblical find of the millennium. They later claimed they were looking for a lost goat or two, but it is just as likely they were doing what curious boys everywhere love to do: explore caves. The first tattered skin rolls with faded scripts that the Bedouin boys found have transformed scholarship for over half a century now, and even if the controversies about what they mean haven't subsided, the discovery story itself is nearly as priceless for history as the scrolls themselves. Known for centuries as Khirbet Qumran ("ruins of Qumran" in Arabic), it isn't hard to imagine how Qumran, near where the scrolls were found, could be considered the end of the world in its desert isolation. This remoteness is true not just for us but even for the Bedouins who lived there in their tents under the shadows of the cliffs, not far from the canyon known in Arabic as Wadi Qumran, or "dry riverbed" of

Qumran. This same remoteness is also a contributing factor why they weren't discovered for so long.

Since being found in 1947, the Dead Sea Scrolls saga reads much like spy fiction rather than truth, and the scrolls are often embroiled in religious and political controversy over their meaning and ownership. Yet this debate over what they mean and who owns them cannot undermine the importance of the documents. Here are a few reasons why the discovery of the Dead Sea Scrolls is acknowledged as one of the most important in history. The ancient scrolls were remarkably well preserved by the aridity of the desert for almost two thousand years, and the discovery story itself is an exciting tale of intrigue and deception. The scrolls contain the oldest biblical manuscript material yet known; their discovery has pushed back our possession and knowledge of biblical manuscripts by more than a thousand years, and the oldest document dates from about 250 BC. They also provide a unique perspective on Jewish religious sects from the first century AD, revealing much more than was previously known. These writings help date ancient material by showing linguistic evolution, and they have been a tempestuous battlefield for modern scholarship. The scrolls were also inextricably connected to Israel's early statehood. The segments of this incredible story can now be woven together in ways that flesh out facts about these scrolls discovered from the caves at Qumran, now much better known as the Dead Sea Scrolls. How the boys actually discovered the texts is something of a debate as well, but their excitement would have been unmistakable and contagious.

How the discovery unfolded

Apparently these two young Bedouin shepherd boys with pounding hearts lay side by side at the top of a cliff one early afternoon. They were flat on their stomachs with barely enough room for both of them to hang over the narrow edge of this desert bluff. Their sandaled feet dug into the rounded cliff and avoided the drop off the dangerously slippery precipice as they peered into the deep blackness below them where a crack, one foot wide, had recently opened up. They didn't know they were probably the first ones to disturb the dust of this Dead Sea cliff for nearly two millennia. One of the boys, Mohammed adh-Dhib, had discovered this crack the day before but had been too afraid to explore by himself so he brought his older cousin back the next day to explore further. But like boys everywhere, daring each other on risky escapades, these boys knew their village relatives and elders would disapprove of their sneaking off. So instead of pretending to herd their goats when they were actually on an adventure, they had tied the herd together and then to a towering rock not too far away.

The desert sun was blinding in the hot blue sky and the dust they stirred up probably made them cough. Dropping nearby pebbles and then rocks down into the hole to gauge its depth, they were surprised to hear distinct ricocheting noises and then what sounded like pottery breaking far below them. Digging only with their small hands, scrabbling at the disintegrating rock with quickly roughening fingernails, they gradually enlarged the crack until it was a sizable gap and the more slender of the two could squeeze down into it with a rope tied around his waist, using his knees and elbows to keep from descending too fast.

By now it was late afternoon and the shadows of the even higher cliffs above them in the dry Wadi Qumran began to lengthen over them. There was barely enough rope for the boy to reach bottom, but he just made it. When his eyes adjusted to the dim light, making sure there were no scorpions or vipers lurking, he gave a shout of triumph and wonder. The full tribal name of this boy was Mohammed Ahmed el-Hamed, but he was nicknamed adh-Dhib, which meant "the Wolf" in the Arabic of his Ta'amireh Bedouin clan. He grabbed a dim handful of the jumbled material from the broken pottery, surprised that some of it crumbled in his grasp. It was too lightweight to be gold or silver treasure, as they had fantasized, but he was still fascinated. He pulled on the rope to ascend and with grunts and wiry strength, the boys together were able to extricate Mohammed from the cave below. They then both climbed up from the slim cliff track and back to more solid ground. As they examined their finds and collected their herd, the sun began to set, and they knew it was time to return home to their village tents. They could better examine their secret discovery by the light of a kerosene lantern after their evening meal when the village elders sat outside around the tents under the starry night and talked. The details of this discovery have been debated for half a century, and perhaps we will never know the exact sequence. The two Bedouin boys didn't know that the treasure they discovered in the Qumran cave was worth far more than any volume of gold they could have imagined.

Since 1947, these hidden desert texts have revolutionized our perceptions of early Jewish and Christian religion; their discovery has, as mentioned, pushed back our possession and knowledge of biblical manuscripts by a thousand years. The accidental finding of the scrolls and the intermittent secrecy of this true story sometimes reads like international intrigue. At other times it reads frustratingly, about a handful of scholars who were determined to keep as much as possible to themselves, using the texts for power and academic advancement.

Mohammed adh-Dhib and his older cousin eventually explored further and then shared their discovery with their village elders, who also retrieved more and more of the fragile texts with ancient writing on them. But it wasn't until a chain of outsiders got involved a few years later that the true significance of the discovery was understood.

The scrolls came to the desert through the dramatic destruction of Jerusalem

In some sense the story of the Dead Sea Scrolls starts as much in Rome as in Jerusalem and the desert nearby, where the scrolls were first hidden away for protection between about AD 66 and 70, when Rome was marching on Jerusalem to quell a Judean rebellion. Judea was only one of several provinces trying to break away during Nero's lax rule as emperor, perhaps thinking Rome was weakening for good. In Rome, with the retirement and death of his wise old adviser Burrus and the forced suicide of his old teacher Seneca, Nero's abuses went unchecked and the empire was now without proper leadership.

Nero preferred racing chariots and his public performances on his kithara, a type of Greek lyre, to actually ruling the Roman empire. These activities were unbecoming to a Roman and even more so to an emperor, according to the historian Tacitus. Nero entirely forsook his imperial duties over the legions, who languished in the provinces. Discipline must have appeared lax to watchful eyes, and word got out to the edges of empire that Rome was disinterested. Within the space of four years between AD 61 and 64, three provinces saw their chance to revolt and did. Queen Boudica stirred up her Britons in the far north of Britannia and burned Roman cities, slaughtering Romans and townsfolk alike in a bid for freedom. Then Caius Julius Civilis led a revolt in Batavia—today the Netherlands; and the simmering eastern province of Judea, always a powder keg under the Jews, who made little attempt to conceal their hatred of the Roman yoke, rebelled under the Sicarii, or Zealots.

Initially, for decades after 1947, it was thought that a sect called the Essenes controlled Qumran, but this is now most unlikely since new excavations at Qumran (1996 onward) have turned up startling results contrary to any isolated, ascetic Essene community intentionally separated from the world. Instead, Qumran appears to have been the fortified desert villa of a wealthy cosmopolitan Jew who had learned from the original Nabatean people how to trap winter storm water in the desert behind earthen dams and divert it to cool deep cisterns where the water stored underground would not evaporate as it would on the surface. This remote location of Qumran was actually more than a stop on the road to the En Gedi oasis. Roman information about the area came from Pliny the Elder, suggesting that Qumran was an extremely arid place no Roman would be likely to venture. This may have been just what some Judeans wanted the Romans to think. At just about the same time Jerusalem was rebelling, Pliny writes:

> To the west of Lake Asphaltitis out of the region of the noxious coastal air lives the solitary Essene tribe, remarkable beyond all others because they have no women and have renounced all sexual desire and wealth and their only living company is the palm tree. Their number grows by means of other refugees from life who join them, having also given up such desires or driven by poverty to such asceticism ... Lying below these Essenes was found in antiquity the desert oasis of En-Gedi.

Pliny was either misinformed about the Essenes or their sites are yet mostly undiscovered. Yet Pliny mentions the balsam trade and other rich products of the Dead Sea. We now know that the oasis of En Gedi was the source of a precious ointment called balsam, secreted as the fragrant healing sap of *opobalsam*, a desert plant unique to En Gedi, and this balsam trade was possibly controlled in part by the owner of the fortified villa at Qumran. The Dead Sea, then called Lake Asphaltitis, was not as barren of life as Pliny suggests, and while it could be seen shimmering from the low buildings of the Qumran plateau, its water was undrinkable. Yet Qumran had ample cistern reservoirs of collected rainwater and was also a pottery production center for Dead Sea products. Rome coveted the Dead Sea region's wealth in the healing balsam industry, famous sweet dates and huge natural resources in medicinal bitumen (used in Egyptian mummification, ship caulking and for pharmaceuticals), and it was most likely for financial gain that the Romans marched to Qumran. But the nearby caves would hardly attract the attention of Roman legions bent on wiping out a political rebellion and appropriating wealth. The caves became the secret location, under the Roman noses, where the Jewish scriptures could be safely hidden. Negotiations from Jerusalem had probably been very quick, and more activity than usual made Qumran a temporary repository of many scrolls rather than just a fortified agrarian villa. Nearby cliffs were riddled with caves because the geology of the eroded plateau was of karstic limestone, a stone that even sparse water could penetrate and dissolve over eons. These caves, mostly invisible from view, would be perfect places to hide sacred treasures until the trouble with Rome blew over.

Sometime between AD 66 and 70, the priests of the Jews lovingly wrapped their sacred writings, some hundreds of years old, along with authoritative commentaries by respected rabbis, and carefully lifted them out of the synagogues around Judea and from the Second Temple itself or its *genizas*, storage places under floors for sacred texts. They placed them in safe hands or, disguised, on merchant carts bound for the desert of Qumran. Perhaps the last oxcarts of hidden documents had just departed the city in AD 70 when highly disciplined Roman legions under Titus, son of Vespasian, closed the last loophole and Jerusalem's great temple roof went up in columns of smoke, as Josephus, the Jewish historian of the first century AD, sadly tells in *Wars of the Jews* (6.5.1):

> While the holy house was on fire, everything was plundered that came to hand . . . The flame was also carried a long way, and made a great noise together with the groans of those who were slain. And because this hill was high and the works of the temple very great, one would have thought the whole city had been on fire.

Possibly looking back at their burning temple, the Jews traveling incognito and in secrecy quickly conducted the treasures of the Law to safety. They could once again affirm (as they had in their Babylonian captivity a half millennium earlier) that their sacred scriptures were more defining of their ancient faith than a mere building, however glorious it had been.

Dead Sea Scroll texts and materials are incredible treasures for biblical scholars

Even though the great number of the separate documents—many only fragmentary—are spread out over centuries and various sects, the actual materials of the Dead Sea Scrolls are fairly uniform and many of the scrolls were originally wrapped in linen for protection. The total number of scrolls varies, depending on whose inventory is used. There are at least 850 scrolls, although it appears to some scholars that this is a conservative number, with perhaps a higher count around 1,000 because of confusion over the possibility of quite a few unpublished documents still being in private hands. Sheepskin was the primary medium and the scribes' ink was a mixture of carbon residue, usually derived from lamp black, and a bit of olive oil or a lubricating agent like a vegetal material of gum arabic or something similar. Because the texts are written in ink, the most likely method of application was by a brush of hairs or even a type of reed quill long used by Egyptian scribes. Although the text is not exactly cursive—what we would think of as written out in longhand with joined letters—but rather brushed letter by individual letter, the letters themselves show rounded edges typical of brushstrokes. Paleographers—who study different scribal hands and writing styles—estimate that up to five hundred different scribes wrote the Dead Sea Scrolls over several hundred years.

The languages of the Dead Sea Scrolls are, in order by volume, Hebrew, Aramaic and Greek. The oldest scrolls are written in Hebrew, itself modified after the Babylonian captivity of around 600 BC into an early form of Aramaized Hebrew. While Aramaic was already a linguistic cousin of Hebrew, this was initially the spoken language they had brought back from Babylonian captivity around 535 BC as the lingua franca, or trade language, of Mesopotamia. The classical Hebrew alphabet, itself borrowed from the Phoenicians, had been altered to the Aramaic one, but over time—in this case a half millennium—the differences between old Hebrew and Aramaized Hebrew and even later Aramaic were not that great, roughly similar to the differences between Shakespearian English and Victorian English.

Although the great majority of ancient texts from Qumran are on sheepskin, one 1952 document, known as 3Q15, stands out because it is made of copper, the so-called Copper Scroll from Cave 3, which is now in two rolled sections. The sheet copper oxidized over two millennia, so it is quite brittle, and it was initially read by X-rays before being carefully sawed and opened up between 1955 and 1956 in a Manchester University laboratory in Britain. The letters were pressed or punched into the sheet copper and its text reveals an inventory of what may have been the Jerusalem temple treasury, smuggled out of the city just before or even during the Roman siege, but most likely not hidden in only one desert location but rather parceled into different caves. One entry on the Copper Scroll (item 10) reads: *In the cavity of the Old House of Tribute, in the Platform of the Chain, 65 bars of gold*. Although the total treasure—and even its very existence—has been debated, this ledger item may have represented a considerable portion of the gold and silver. At least sixty-five caches or treasure deposits are enumerated in the scroll. But this treasure has never been found or, if it has, never been made public. More than a few adventurers have searched the desert for it, in the hopes that the treasure itself still lies in a cave somewhere.

Before the Dead Sea Scrolls, the oldest Jewish scriptural manuscripts dated back only a thousand years to the Middle Ages, and were mostly copied by a group called Masoretes. The oldest previous biblical collections were the Aleppo Codex, also called the Keter Aram Tzova and vocalized by Ben Asher in AD 920, although it is not a complete collection of Hebrew scripture, followed by the Leningrad Codex, also dated to the tenth century AD. Rather than being a scroll, a codex is an early book of groups of pages sewn together. The previous oldest single manuscript fragment of Jewish scripture was the Nash Papyrus, a small Egyptian fragment of the Ten Commandments from around 100 BC. After this, the oldest complete Old Testament Christian codices were the Codex Sinaiticus and Codex Alexandrinus in the British Library, both fourth century AD.

As mentioned, the Dead Sea discovery pushed written text dates back to more than a thousand years earlier, circa AD 70 and in some cases a few centuries earlier to the second century BC, enabling scholars to understand how many texts were copied virtually unchanged over centuries. The drama of the discovery and decipherment of these scrolls crosses three continents and reads like a saga of national pride as well as espionage, as several intelligence services were employed to track down and buy material from assorted collections of these precious scrolls. How different cultures, religions and nations wrestled over these desert fragments for fifty years is a story worthy of attention.

The story after 1947 made politics and religion uneasy bedfellows

Politics and religion are not conducive to archaeological research. In total there are eleven major Qumran caves. Since 1947, the caves of Qumran have yielded many hundreds of scrolls, the majority of which are fragmentary, but some caves, like Cave 4, probably discovered in 1952, produced up to almost four hundred scroll texts alone, about 40 percent of the total volume known, a number of which were intact in the same kind of clay jars. In addition to the original Cave 1 discovered by Mohammed adh-Dhib on the bluff, and the enormously rich Cave 4 adjacent to it, about eight feet wide and twenty feet long, other caves along

the cliffs and above the wadi have proved that the whole canyon
and the surrounding region of up to several square miles were all
used for safekeeping these vital documents at the heart of ancient
Judaism.

The story is murky and there are many side trails that are
hard to track, but the main narrative must run something like
this. In late spring of 1947 after the Ta'amireh Bedouin tribe
found enough scrolls to warrant their curiosity, their elders took
at least four scrolls from Cave 1 either directly to Bethlehem or
indirectly through a local sheikh, hoping an antiquities dealer
named Khalil Iskander Shahin, locally known as Kando, could
give them a bit of money for their finds. Kando dealt mostly in
illicit ancient pottery or the kind of pilgrim relics and souvenirs
one could then still find around Bethlehem, and he couldn't read
the texts.

But Kando was shrewd, and he knew these tattered skins
were old enough to sell to someone who treasured such things.
He brought in another friend, George Isaiah, who probably
helped to squirrel such things out from under the not-so-watch-
ful eyes of the British Mandate authorities, who were more
concerned with the incendiary politics of feuding Palestine than
a few old skins. Both Kando and George Isaiah were members
of the Syrian Orthodox Church and, rather than report and turn
in their finds to the Rockefeller Museum in East Jerusalem as
law required, they instead negotiated through contacts within
their church in Old Jerusalem, correctly surmising they would
never see the documents again and lose any possible sale if they
followed the letter of the law. These scrolls now came to the
attention of the Syrian archbishop, Athanasius Yeshua Samuel,
whose ecclesiastic office gave him near autonomy over his Jerusalem diocese.

Although he was anything but a scholar, more a church bureaucrat and unable to read Hebrew or Aramaic, Archbishop Samuel sensed these documents were valuable because his monastery had a library of old manuscripts. Through Kando and George Isaiah, the archbishop requested the Bedouin bring whatever they had to the Monastery of St. Mark, where he presided. Apparently they came, bringing more scrolls than anyone expected—possibly eight to ten—but there was a communications breakdown and the unannounced Bedouin were turned away. This was not surprising, given both their and the monastery gatekeeper's obvious mistrust of outsiders, the local political turmoil, and the Bedouins' "uncouth" desert appearance.

Kando managed to salvage something of the stymied sale from the angry Bedouin, buying four scrolls, all apparently from Cave 1. This first cache turned out to be an incredible treasure. Not only was one scroll an entire book of Isaiah, measuring twenty-four feet long, but there was also the Habakkuk Pesher (a commentary on the biblical book of Habakkuk) and the Genesis Apocryphon, as they are known today. Considering their pricelessness to history, the low price the Syrian church paid to Kando is still amazing: only twenty-four British pounds. The Bedouin probably received only a fraction of that paltry sum.

Archbishop Samuel, now encouraged by his own manuscript acquisition, commissioned George Isaiah and a priest to conduct their own illegal archaeological dig at Qumran, having found out this was the provenance of the scrolls. It is impossible to determine what George Isaiah found in mid 1947, but ultimately these first four scrolls acquired from the Bedouin were brought for consultation to Syria and the Damascus–Homs region, where the patriarch of the Syrian Jacobite Church presided over the larger church headquarters. Apparently permission was given to proceed with the illegal desert excavations, since the scrolls seemed to have returned to Jerusalem and the St. Mark's monastery. In Jerusalem, Archbishop Samuel sought clandestine advice from Hebrew scholars, including Professor Eleazar Sukenik, who headed the Archaeology Department at the new Hebrew University. This was dangerous and difficult because Jerusalem was heavily partitioned. Several visits were necessary between Sukenik and intermediaries at the monastery, and finally Sukenik himself went incognito to Bethlehem in late November. This was a very dangerous trip because Jews, Muslims and Christian Palestinians were all in a state of constant uproar over the frequent abductions and murders of soldiers (even British "peacekeepers") and citizens alike in dark alleys and even public places where hotheaded factions patrolled the walled-up sectors of Jerusalem. Bethlehem was definitely "enemy" territory for Sukenik.

Professor Sukenik was able to verify the authenticity of the scrolls and just after he returned to Jerusalem, the newly formed United Nations by a majority vote established the formation of the State of Israel. The historic value of the scrolls from Cave 1 was now dramatically enhanced by a coincidence of great historic proportions: just as the scrolls had been placed for safekeeping in Judean caves two millennia before, when Judea and its Jews were about to be destroyed by Rome, so a resurrected state for Jews was now capable of finding its own past in biblical writings.

Having hurriedly found means to buy this portion of the scrolls from the Syrians, Sukenik haggled and made an offer. But his offer was put off for a week, during which time the archbishop had found a better price, offered by the Americans through Professor William F. Albright from Johns Hopkins University and the American School of Oriental Research in Jerusalem (renamed in honor of Albright in 1970). Given the increasing instability in Jerusalem, the scrolls were taken first to Beirut and then New York for storage in a bank vault to await the imminent purchase.

The discovery then went public in the United States. In April 1948, Yale University's spokesperson was Professor Millar Burrows, who was director of both Yale's Department of Near Eastern Languages as well as the American School of Oriental Research's Jerusalem Institute. The press release in the *New York Times* on April 11, 1948, excerpted here, was hardly dramatic at the time:

> the earliest known manuscript of the Book of *Isaiah* . . . was found in the Syrian monastery of St. Mark in Jerusalem, where it had been preserved in a scroll of parchment dating to about the first century BC. Recently it was identified by scholars of the American School of Oriental Research at Jerusalem.

Also mentioning other Hebrew scrolls, the press release deliberately obscured if not outright manipulated the exact find location. Burrows's statement was a half-truth because while the manuscripts were now the property of the Syrian Monastery of St. Mark, their cave source was kept secret for fear of others ransacking the desert at Qumran. It is likely that this was what Archbishop Samuel and his agents told the Oriental Institute, which had sufficient resources to undertake its own excavations even in the political hot potato of Palestine. The press release hardly caused a ripple in the news of rising turmoil in Palestine.

In 1948, backed by increasingly sympathetic United Nations resolutions, Israel had declared its independence and an immediate war ensued between Israel and the surrounding Arab states. The hostilities between the fledgling state and its neighbors were fed by invading troops hailing not only from adjacent Egypt, Transjordan, Syria and Lebanon but also Saudi Arabia and Iraq. It wasn't until January 1949 that hostilities ended with a negotiated cease-fire. Transjordan now changed its name to Jordan, and Jerusalem was divided in half between Israel and Jordan. Qumran and the Dead Sea region was under the jurisdiction of Jordan, and was to remain so for almost two decades.

Father Roland de Vaux was the director of the Ecole Biblique but not an archaeologist by training. De Vaux was also the primary proponent of the Essene community theory. He proceeded to work with the British expatriate and Jordanian director of antiquities, Gerald Lankester Harding, in excavating the ruins of Qumran itself in 1951. They produced a survey of all caves and possible sites—over 270—in the area. They also turned up more scroll material, as well as finding the Copper Scroll in Cave 3 in 1952. Cave 4, perhaps the richest of all Dead Sea Scroll caves, was discovered and excavated in 1952. Naturally, the same Ta'amireh Bedouin tribesmen who had found the first material were again involved in the actual digging and cave exploration. All of the scroll material acquired by excavations at Qumran under Jordanian auspices between 1951 and 1953 was organized and categorized. The material was housed in the Rockefeller Museum in Jerusalem by 1955 but removed to a bank vault in Amman, Jordan, during the Suez Crisis in 1956 and not returned to the Rockefeller Museum—somewhat the worse for wear—until 1957. In 1966, although it had been an independent and international institution, the Rockefeller Museum was nationalized by Jordan, and the resident scrolls from Qumran officially became Jordanian property.

The story now becomes even more convoluted. Professor Eleazer Sukenik had a tactically brilliant son who renamed himself Yigael Yadin, a Hebrew name, rather than keep his

European surname of Sukenik. Yadin had resigned his post in the Israeli Defense Force in 1949 and went on to study archaeology at Hebrew University, earning a Ph.D. on the Dead Sea Scrolls.

Despite the initial clamor of publicity, intended to escalate a bidding war, back in the Syrian Orthodox community, the sale of the three scrolls held by Archbishop Samuel had stalled for several reasons during the years since 1948. The potential American buyers had backed down because Jordan had claimed that the scrolls held by the Syrian church were stolen property from Qumran. Now that the asking price had deteriorated to a measly half million dollars in 1954 from the original million dollars, Yadin made disguised efforts to purchase the three scrolls from the Syrian Orthodox Church through intermediaries. This was necessary because Jordan and the Syrian church would have strenuously objected if it were openly known that Israel was the only real potential buyer. Jordan would have been irate on diplomatic grounds because it was still smarting from the war, when it lost part of west Palestine on the other side of the Jordan River. The Syrians could balk on religious grounds because they were a Christian entity, preferring that their three published scrolls and a fourth that had not been published would soon belong to Christians of some persuasion rather than Jews.

Yadin now made perhaps his most brilliant strategic move in the chesslike game of high stakes with the scrolls. He invented a story of a man named "Mr. Green" to conceal Israeli involvement and possession of the scrolls, and this ruse was unknown to the Syrian Christians at the time. In New York, Yadin worked through a local banker to negotiate with the Syrians and found another anonymous benefactor to provide the money. An agreed-upon low price of $250,000 transferred hands between the Syrian church and intermediaries after the mysterious "Mr. Green" guaranteed the four scrolls' authenticity. "Mr. Green" was actually

Professor Harry Orlinsky, an American scholar of Hebrew. The following day the four scrolls were transferred from the bank to the Waldorf-Astoria's hotel vault and removed quietly and quickly to the Israeli Consulate in New York before anyone could object. The scrolls traveled secretly and independently of each other to Israel. Yadin returned to Jerusalem after communicating in code during the whole journey about the whereabouts of his acquisition, a major diplomatic coup for Israel.

In 1967 war broke out between Jordan and Israel. During this rapid Six Days' War in 1967, the Israelis took the rest of Jerusalem and occupied the Rockefeller Museum. The museum now faced Israeli appropriation of the scroll materials it held, amid the mounting anger of the Ecole Biblique. The political climate in Jerusalem, where Israel now occupied Jordan's eastern half of the city, made 1967 a very different time. Father de Vaux feared that Israel would manipulate its conquest of Jerusalem to sequester all the scrolls housed there. This was partly because in the years since 1951, he had refused any requests of Jews to work on the scrolls. Perhaps to keep peace with a new population of Palestinians in East Jerusalem, Israel left the research and publication of Cave 4's enormous material of around eight hundred scrolls to the Ecole Biblique and its team. But Israel considered the Cave 4 scrolls its property as spoils of war, whereas the Ecole Biblique group working in the Rockefeller Museum continued to resist Israeli participation in what it perceived as its personal scroll collection.

Finally making the Dead Sea Scrolls public was a great coup

For decades the international Dead Sea Scrolls team, dominated by the Ecole Biblique, eked out a few fragments a year and blocked efforts of every outside biblical scholar and archaeologist, myself included, to conduct research on the scrolls under their aegis. Requests by distinguished Hebrew scholars were turned down dozens of times by the parochial Ecole Biblique team or their successors in the United States and elsewhere. Finally, in 1991, the Ecole Biblique–dominated "cabal" was dramatically broken.

There were several precipitating causes. First, Hershel Shanks, the tenacious publisher of *Biblical Archaeology Review* (*BAR*) and *Bible Review* in Washington, DC, had been pushing the international team of a dozen or so scholars to either speed up their painfully slow publication rate to keep pace with the Israelis, whose scrolls were fully published, or turn over the huge volume of material to younger scholars worldwide. Shanks was met with silence for several years and snubbed professionally. In 1989, the Israel Archaeological Council assumed oversight of the huge amount of unpublished Qumran Cave 4 material being held by the international Dead Sea Scrolls team, including those in the hands of scholars abroad. The Israeli council issued an ultimatum for quicker publication. It was agreed upon but effectively ignored through John Strugnell, Dead Sea Scrolls team director.

Then in 1985 Shanks launched a publicity campaign through *BAR* to break through the publication barriers. Shanks finally determined that the Rockefeller Museum had made complete photographs of all the scrolls and fragments in their collection almost fifty years previously. Back in the 1960s the Ecole Biblique had given permission to the Rockefeller to take the photographs because Jerusalem was not considered the safest place for their survival. The microfilm negatives went to faraway San Marcos, California, to be placed in the vaults of the Huntington Library for safekeeping.

Shanks first published in *BAR* an unauthorized set of facsimile documents, and the international Dead Seas Scrolls team threatened a lawsuit, which hardly fazed this lawyer-turned-publisher. Shanks then persuaded the Huntington Library's director, Dr. William A. Moffett, to release the Dead Sea Scrolls photographic negatives for publication, which the Huntington's prescient board of directors saw as in the best public interest. This was announced on September 22, 1991, to extensive media coverage. The secrecy dam was finally broken, once and for all.

The second unpredictable tumult that broke the publishing monopoly of the Cave 4 material (40 percent of the total texts) unfolded in a sadly unpredictable event. An unwell John Strugnell had publicly declared in what he miscalculated was a private venue that Judaism was nothing more than a reaction against Christianity. This outrageous comment was published in the *New York Times*, followed by an enormous public outcry. Within two days, Strugnell, already mostly retired, was summarily dismissed from his post as project director for the international team, and the Israelis swiftly consolidated all the control of the Dead Sea Scrolls documents and fragments under one oversight, stripping the parochial remnant faction of exclusive rights to hold back or monopolistically publish their trove. In one move, Israel accomplished what Father Roland de Vaux had feared most years before: the new director of the Dead Sea Scrolls project was an Israeli, Emanuel Tov of Hebrew University. The fifty years of stonewalling and parochialism was over. The control of a group who thought only they knew best, who had kept the bulk of the Dead Sea Scrolls to themselves, keeping the world guessing wildly about the contents and their ramifications, was now broken forever.

Since 1991, a multitude of books have summarized, published or compiled Dead Sea Scrolls material. In microfiche form, all the Dead Sea Scrolls photos have also been published by the Israel Antiquities Authority in conjunction with Brill Press in 1993, but not all are translated as of 2007. The exact volume of yet-untranslated material is unknown, partly because there is still an unverifiable amount of Dead Sea Scrolls documents in private hands. The usual assessment is that this untranslated material is less than 1 percent of the total volume of Dead Sea Scrolls. It is likely that debates about the meaning of the scrolls will rage for at least another half century or more, but there is consensus that they are of vital importance to biblical studies and archaeology.

The texts represent both religious and secular writing over centuries

The Dead Sea Scrolls documents have been given an alphanumeric descriptive code based on where they were found, although a few are still without this context, having derived from the illegal antiquities market. For example, the designation of 1Q means that the document was from Cave 1 at Qumran. The texts are also categorized separately by subject, as shown below, into biblical and nonbiblical material. While most are fragmentary, at least one scroll is remarkably well preserved apparently in near entirety: this is the so-called Temple Scroll (11Q19–20) from Cave 11 at Qumran. The longest document of the group, it is 26.7 feet long, but some have suggested that it was originally almost 2 feet longer.

The subject categories of the Dead Sea Scrolls include:

Scripture (e.g., Torah; Law, as in Genesis and Nevi'im; Prophets, as in Isaiah and Toledot; Generations or Histories, as in 2 Samuel and Ketubim; Writings, as in Psalms). Nearly every biblical book in the Jewish canon is represented and at least one whole book, that of Isaiah, is preserved among other books on one scroll. Every Old Testament book except Esther is represented at least in part and many biblical books exist almost in their entirety, such as Psalms, Deuteronomy, Genesis and Isaiah.

Commentaries (e.g., Talmud, Targums, Pesherim, or Mishnah). These are usually rabbinical writings about scripture (but can also be nonrabbinic) and contain many individual biblical text references to scripture.

Apocalyptic/Apocryphal/Pseudepigraphic (e.g., War Scroll, Damascus Scroll, Community Rule). These are mostly religious texts that include rules and observances for the community as well as writings about impending judgment. These also include texts that were rejected from canonic scripture but are nonetheless valuable, as well as texts claimed to be written by known or legendary biblical individuals. Divination and magic texts also fall under this category. This is perhaps the most interesting of all Dead Sea Scrolls material because it sheds light on an otherwise unknown body of religious observances that is otherwise absent from Judaism.

Documents (e.g., Copper Scroll). These are not religious texts but items identifying accounting and inventories of treasure. Sometimes contemporary correspondence fits in this category as well.

The overall umbrella of the term Dead Sea Scrolls has been enlarged to allow for Greek as well as Aramaic and Hebrew language. The materials include leather and papyrus but the greatest majority, at least 98 percent of the Dead Sea Scrolls corpus, is written in ink on sheepskin and in the contemporary language of Aramaic or Aramaized Hebrew. The dating of some of the material is much older than the time of the Jerusalem destruction around AD 70. For example, the Isaiah Scroll, which some arguably date to about 250 BC, appears the oldest. The great majority, however, date to the middle of the first century AD, around the time of the Jewish rebellion against Rome, just before they were hidden from certain destruction.

Despite conspiracy theories, the scrolls do not easily connect to Christianity

To date no verifiable New Testament material has been discovered, which supports the fact that it was a Jewish community that hid the texts. It also highlights the historically accepted perception that Christian texts hardly existed at this time. This obviously leads to controversy about the texts. Many have sought in vain to find Christian connections in the Dead Sea Scrolls or references to Jesus, but they apparently do not exist. While a few have also tried to connect the New Testament person of John the Baptist to the Essene community because the gospels portray him as ascetic, this conjecture is also without any evidence. The closest parallel to Christianity may be that one religious leader of the Essenes or the Qumran community appears to have been led by a mysterious figure called the Teacher of Righteousness. At least a few Christian scholars have tried to claim this person follows a precedent set by Jesus, however unlikely this might be.

Conspiracy theories are nothing new, but because the international Dead Sea Scrolls team, originally assembled around 1950 by the Ecole Biblique and others, maintained an atmosphere of high-handed control over the bulk of their documents for almost fifty years, not all scholars are completely convinced that there isn't some collusion yet to be revealed.

For years rumors abounded about the contents of many of the scrolls, leading to many unfounded conspiracy theories. This was mostly due to the deliberate blocking of access to outsiders and the monopolistic snail's pace of publication of Cave 4 Qumran material. One rumor even had it that the Vatican was suppressing the scrolls' publication because some of their contents would undermine Roman Catholicism and its dogmatic version of early Christianity. While understandable, given the reprehensible secrecy and tightfistedness of this team (many of whom were not even trained as translators), this is absurd because Christianity appears not to be mentioned. Others have long rumored that some of the texts made reference to Jesus and New Testament activities but that such references were destroyed or expunged. One such popular book published in the late 1980s, titled *Jesus and the Secret of the Dead Sea Scrolls*, was clearly marketed for an audience created out of the hype over the absence of published Cave 4 material. In other rumors, modern Jews were said to have suppressed publication because it would destroy official positions about ancient Judaism. This is also unreasonable given that the then mostly secular state of modern Israel actively pursued publication of all the texts it possessed and constantly pushed the others who controlled texts to publish their portions.

Such views about New Testament or Christian connections are highly doubtful for several reasons. The first argument against this position is the fact that for nearly five decades, from around 1950 to 1990, at least 40 percent of extant texts, all from Cave 4, were held within the control of the French Roman Catholic Dominicans of the Ecole Biblique in Jerusalem or their handpicked Christian successors. If verifiable New Testament material existed, they most likely would have hailed it as fundamental to understanding early Christian beginnings. As such, the unique religious community material appears to bridge late Judaism of the first century and New Testament gospels mostly in that our knowledge of this hitherto-unknown Jewish sect—possibly Essene but not necessarily so—is now greatly enlarged. The second primary argument against this rumor of Christian connections is that because Jerusalem at the time of destruction was overwhelmingly populated by religious Jews of traditional Judaism, they would hardly be sympathetic to hiding Christian writings they would consider heretical alongside their own biblical texts.

Naturally, as already mentioned, Christianity at the time hardly had anything canonically identified as scriptures anyway, and Paul's epistles were clearly perceived as anti-Judaic and pro-Gentile in the minds of those who treasured their Judaic heritage. The third argument against all these rumors comes from the advantage of hindsight. Now that the majority of texts are published, translated and identified (less than 15 percent remaining unidentified), no revolutionary material has emerged supporting these rumors or conspiracy theories, and it is clear that these are primarily Jewish documents hidden from the conquering Romans.

Conclusion

The Dead Sea Scrolls have provided the oldest biblical documents known as well as a clearer picture of Judaism in the first century AD. They tell us much about the text parallels between biblical books of the Jewish scriptures before they were adopted by Christianity as the Old Testament and much about writing and scribal practices of the first century.

In the aftermath of making the Dead Sea Scrolls accessible to all in 1991, it is hard to understand why one small group was so obsessed with controlling the scrolls. Perhaps it was motivated only by academic exclusivity—the desire to control an intellectual fiefdom. Perhaps the rigid control and delays in publication were caused by sectarian pride, or dogma and fear wrangling over potential misinterpretations, apostasy or resurrected heresies. Yet neither Christianity nor Judaism has been destroyed as a result of publication.

Nearly all the surviving Dead Sea Scrolls in public hands are now available to anyone on DVD or microfilm, and many are now online as well. While the controversies around the withholding of material will eventually subside, the arguable interpretations will continue to unfold over decades and even centuries to come. Whatever the outcome, the concept of a biblical treasure of such historic proportions would have been inconceivable to the two Bedouin boys of 1947, to whose curiosity we will be forever in debt.

Chapter 8

Thera
The Key to the Aegean Bronze Age

Aegean Sea, 1967

The archaeologist shielded his weathered face against the afternoon sun reflecting off the Aegean. He wasn't young anymore; in fact, he knew that now in his sixties he was old to be leading a rigorous new field project that would tire even much younger men. But he had been carefully assembling his data for decades on this little island of Thera. This dig was his final testing grounds for a theory many had scorned for years. After training in Minoan archaeology for long seasons, and leading projects on Crete, this patient archaeologist, Spyridon Marinatos, knew he needed to find something dramatic to vindicate his scholarship once and for all. Did he know this would be the day? Possibly. He had waited decades to find just the right spot, and this one already had some telltale signs—small broken potsherds emerging from just several feet below the surface on only the second day of digging. His local workers, from the nearby village of Akrotiri, were now trained to handle carefully anything that came up in their shovels and trowels in the soft, fine volcanic ash that powdered their clothes white and stuck to everything.

It was the shout of excitement from the middle of the deepening trench that made his heart beat suddenly faster. He hurried over a few yards to examine what the worker was holding up gingerly in one hand while brushing it off with the other. Judging from its large silhouette, clearly this was not just another fragment. Dropping down on his knees, Marinatos's experienced eyes gleamed as he quickly scanned and recognized the shape of a complete clay vessel. Thrilled, he saw the graceful ceramic vase was a beautifully intact, perfectly preserved Minoan stirrup vase, but then, blowing the dusty ash from the vase surface, his breath was taken away. The elegant vessel had a unique decoration of blue on white, a dolphin motif unlike any Minoan decoration he knew. Given the many sea miles of distance from Crete, this combination of known shape and unknown decoration was an extremely important hallmark. Eureka! He knew he had finally found the proof that he'd waited so long to uncover. . . . Even if this event is reconstructed from correspondence, conversations, and memories of witnesses, however trustworthy, its essence is still confirmed by Marinatos's exciting discovery.

Beyond the rewarding story of Marinatos's dogged determination and instinct honed by years of preparation, the site of Akrotiri on Thera is very important for a number of reasons. Here Marinatos and his younger fellow archaeologist Christos Doumas soon uncovered a whole city buried by volcanic eruption, and the destruction of Thera now appears to help date the transition between the Middle and Late Bronze Ages. The eruption may have also destroyed a considerable part of the Minoan fleet on Crete, with a wide path of its ash spreading all the way to Palestine, and probably seriously affected Minoan civilization. Additionally, Thera's rich trade with Egypt, including shipping olive oil from the Greek mainland, also centered on valuable local items like emery. In its multiple-storied buildings, many still standing, Akrotiri's preserved wall frescoes show the high level of art and civilization on the island. Ultimately, Akrotiri may even prove Plato's long-lost Atlantis is not just a myth. While Atlantis may never be understood, it is possible that Thera and the discovery of Akrotiri hold the key to understanding not only Atlantis but Aegean trade at a vital juncture of ancient history, possibly even ending one age and ushering in another, around 1620 BC.

Even now Thera is perhaps the most beautiful island in the sparkling blue Aegean Sea. Thanks to years of study since Marinatos began digging at Akrotiri, we know it was even more so in antiquity. Visible for many miles away, its perfectly shaped cone mountain rose high above the shining water. Forests climbed its slopes, and its old legendary name brought awe to all who knew it or had traveled there in the eastern Mediterranean. Some knew this island as Kalliste, the "Fairest Isle," and a growing number of archaeologists and ancient historians now believe it was the source of the myth of Atlantis. People today, sailing boats around its capes or peering down into the deep waters where the light reaches, call the island Thera or Santorini. It rests serenely alone in the Aegean Sea between mainland Greece and Crete almost away from sight of all the other islands. Today divers go deep into the clear water where sponges grow or where octopus colonies hide under the rocks. But the island we see now is very different from what it looked like before 1620 BC, when it was truly spectacular. Now it is only a shadow of its former beauty. This is because a world-changing volcanic eruption blew up most of the island around 3,400 years ago, leaving only a thin crescent of land and a deep caldera crater. Deep water now fills in what once was a round island. Was the island of Thera truly Atlantis?

Spyridon Marinatos (1901–74) was one of the first modern historians to seriously consider the importance of ancient Thera. In 1939 he shook up the conservative academic community with a lecture and a paper published in the respected journal *Antiquity* that raised the possibility that the volcanic destruction of ancient Thera might have brought about the end of the Minoan civilization. Others have followed Marinatos by connecting Thera with the mythical Atlantis, both of them destroyed by nature in the forgotten past. At the time, much of the scholarly world laughed at Marinatos, and he had to wait almost forty years to truly test his hypothesis with an excavation on Thera. History and his successor, Christos Doumas, have proven that Spyridon Marinatos was absolutely right about a massive destruction that altered civilization in the Aegean. When he excavated on ancient Thera, he dramatically discovered the lost city of Akrotiri, a city buried in ash. As archaeologist Colin Renfrew said in 1983, "Thera . . . must rank as the most completely preserved prehistoric site in Europe, perhaps in the world."

Akrotiri may prove Plato's long-lost Atlantis is not just a myth

If the story of Atlantis is true—and Plato seemed to believe it—Atlantis was also very likely a great ancient civilization that ruled the seas before it was destroyed by a huge cataclysm. Linking Atlantis to Thera is still a very controversial idea, but here is the core of what Plato wrote sometime in the first half of the fourth century BC about Atlantis (Timaeus 25a–d):

> Now in this island of Atlantis there was a great and wonderful empire which had rule over the whole island and several

others, and over parts of the continent, and, furthermore, the men of Atlantis had subjected the parts of Libya within the columns of Heracles as far as Egypt, and of Europe as far as Tyrrhenia . . . . But afterwards there occurred violent earthquakes and floods; and in a single day and night of misfortune all your warlike men in a body sank into the earth, and the island of Atlantis in like manner disappeared in the depths of the sea. For which reason the sea in those parts is impassable and impenetrable, because there is a shoal of mud in the way; and this was caused by the subsidence of the island.

If we examine Plato's excerpted words on Atlantis, maybe through the eyes of Marinatos, several things immediately stand out. First, according to Plato, Atlantis was not just one island but an island empire, which required it to be a maritime power ruling the sea and the islands in it as well as much of the land around it. This would involve many ships and great navigational skills. What we now know is that long-distance oversea trade had been around for millennia in the Aegean, linking Europe to Egypt and the coast of Palestine by water over considerable distances of hundreds of miles.

Evidence for this early maritime trade has been found through the work of archaeologists like Colin Renfrew, who helped prove decades ago that obsidian was traded across the Aegean from islands like Melos to the Greek mainland and even to Anatolia (Turkey) as far back as six thousand years ago. Other archaeologists, such as Peter Warren, have studied diorite stone vases from Egypt, carved long before that land was united, as far back as 3000 BC or earlier. These predynastic Egyptian vessels ended up on the island of Crete at some undetermined later date.

Aegean and Mediterranean sea trade would require sailing out of sight of land, a frightening prospect for most of human history. Lionel Casson, the world's foremost authority on ancient seafaring, suggests this Mediterranean scenario is not at all far-fetched. This is because navigators long relied on the positions of the sun, moon and stars for sighting and, after long observations, they were also able to predict the seasons of favorable winds. The ancient sailors depended on careful observations and generations of experience because the variable sea could never really be mastered. They knew that the wide sea could just as easily end their lives as bring them almost unimaginable wealth through trade. Yet many braved the sea by crossing again and again, considering the opportunities greater than the risks. If enough ships were built and sailed or rowed, filled with men to police the water traffic in the sea lanes or harbors, it is completely possible that one civilization could have controlled commerce and travel. So Plato is right in the sense that a culture or civilization could have ruled the seas, and many scholars do suggest that during 1800 to 1500 BC, the Minoans of Crete ruled the seafaring world in the eastern Mediterranean between Greece and Egypt.

Another thing we can take from Plato's words is that his account of the physical destruction of Atlantis is very close to what would have transpired in a volcanic eruption, often preceded and accompanied by earthquakes. The description could have been written from an observer's view from very close to the eruption, wherein much would have been obscured by clouds of ash and steam generated by boiling seawater. Equally, an observer could have been viewing from miles away if the same phenomena spread out for miles around this Aegean area. These phenomena would likely have been attributed to the traumatic earthquakes often assigned to Poseidon, god of the sea. Plato's story, differing slightly from a firsthand observation of a volcanic eruption but recorded just as seen or heard from a safer distance, could have been passed down orally through many generations until someone wrote it down. Furthermore, the island's disappearance by subsidence, just as Plato noted, is quite in keeping with Thera having blown up, with the bulk of it, perhaps over 80 percent, disappearing as water rushed in to fill the deep caldera crater. The shoals Plato mentioned are absent today from Thera, but there are remnants of a circle of low island fragments around the caldera, and a new island, Nea Kameni, emerged near the center of the sea crater from modern volcanic activity between 1707 and 1950.

In all, Plato's description of the destruction of Atlantis is uncannily close to what would have been observable from any ships fleeing Thera. Some survivors—later telling their frightening stories to their offspring—must have been lucky enough to escape just in time from ancient Thera's buried harbor at Akrotiri or other harbors completely destroyed, along with most of the people who lived along them.

The Greek seismologist Angelos Galanopoulos took Marinatos one step further in 1960 by theorizing that Thera's destruction was directly associated with the myth of Atlantis and its demise. As time goes on, thanks to plausible collaborative reconstructions by volcanologists and archaeologists, some in the academic world no longer consider Atlantis just a myth repeated by Plato. Atlantis does not need to remain an elaborate tale relegated to speculation, but was possibly a real place whose rise and demise may be historically validated in Thera. On the other hand, Thera's destruction is not necessarily connected to the end of Minoan culture but is nonetheless—even if only a local microcosm representing the mythic demise of Atlantis—vastly important in its own right as a major Cycladic island entrepôt.

Marinatos and Doumas uncovered a whole city buried by the volcanic eruption

The facts of the destruction of Thera can be reconstructed from what remains. Of the group of fragmentary islands surrounding the volcanic caldera, the primary remnant island, Thera, having partly survived the Bronze Age eruption around 1620 BC, now circles the deep water of the sunken crater like a crescent moon facing west. The secondary remnant island is Therasia, on the west side of the caldera mouth. Thera has the steep walls of a volcanic throat on the inner west side of the main island crescent that faces the caldera. This volcanic circle is a high cliff almost a thousand feet high in places. In contrast, the outer east side tapers off, usually leveling off gently to the water, although peaks like Profitis Ilias (Prophet Elijah) jut out from the flat landscape up to some 2,600 feet high. These surviving peaks are probably nowhere near the height of the original island volcanic cone. The older small island in the middle of the caldera, now called Palaia (Old) Kameni, was thought to have most likely erupted from the sea. This account can be found in the writing of the Greek geographer Strabo around AD 20, although written a few hundred years after the fact, since Old Kameni rose from the sea near Thera around 197 BC.

The archaeological site of Akrotiri, the main Bronze Age site left on the island, lies on the south end of the crescent of land, close to the sea, sheltered from the north and northwest winds that blow almost all the time across the sea and over the island. This city once had a protected harbor where ships could berth from wind and storm. One can imagine even greater shelter from prevailing bad weather when the volcanic peak slightly to the north rose high above the town. This was before the eruption blew away three-quarters of the island mass and much of what was left collapsed into the deep caldera seen today. Only about twenty-eight square miles is left of over a likely one hundred or more square miles. A thick layer of ash covered the bulk of the island from the 1620 BC eruption, seen in some places as three separate strata from 60 to 150 feet or more thick, and it was at least 30 to 40 feet deep at Akrotiri itself.

Although Marinatos had to wait over a quarter century—partly due to two intervening wars—for vindication of his ideas about the connection of Thera's volcanic demise to the collapse of a civilization, in the interim he was carefully assembling clues about where to find the best location for evidence. He was helped in this by previous nineteenth-century research. First, between 1870 and 1874, the early French excavator H. Mamet had started an exploratory search at a ravine adjacent to Favatas near Akrotiri. Mamet had found white slip pottery from Cyprus, proving trade with other distant islands in the Minoan period. The German Archaeological Institute in Athens also provided Marinatos with records of its early exploration, among them the Kamaras site along the Potamos valley. In addition, Baron Hiller von Gaertringen had also done work at a hillside site of classical Thera, itself 1,300 feet above sea level on the Mesa Vouno hill in 1890, and he had also overseen the various surveys of his assistant R. Zahn in different places across the island.

Marinatos learned from the archaeological archives and from old farmers in that part of the island that his predecessors Mamet and Zahn had turned up a significant amount of broken "Minoan" pottery along the Potamos valley, especially near Favatas, opposite Akrotiri. Prehistoric giant stone mortars still being used by the townspeople of Favatas helped confirm its importance to Marinatos. He accurately reasoned these mill-stones were too large and heavy to move any great distance. The final clue came from farmers' reports of collapsing earth in several places around this same area of the Potamos valley and its ravine. Marinatos suspected at once that this collapsing ground was proof of cavities under the surface, indicating collapsing roof structures under the surface ash layers. Adding up all the background data of ancient ceramic finds of a sufficiently high density in one spot—suggesting to an archaeologist some kind of long-term settlement—along with the pioneering reports of his predecessors, Marinatos was persuaded that he was looking in exactly the right place to find a lost city. Marinatos must have walked many times over the low plateau and coastal hills around the Potamos valley, seeing the fine volcanic dust covering the island's surface being picked up by the sea breeze from the north and wondering what lay beneath.

We can only imagine Marinatos's excitement in 1967 when, after barely breaking through the fine ash on the surface, his first explorations near the surface immediately turned up Minoan-style pottery in dense clusters. Marinatos presided over that first season at Akrotiri. His first daunting task was having to move the tons of fine ash that poured like sand over the deepening steep side walls of his dig as he descended. He quickly struck ancient stone walls and window and door lintels of major architectural structures and knew he had found something unique and special. Christos Doumas joined him in 1968 to assist in the excavation and continued through to the turn of the millennium.

Their joint Akrotiri venture between 1967 and 1974 yielded a whole city, revealing block after block of two- and three-story houses with narrow streets set around public squares. So far, over 2.5 acres of city have been excavated without any clear sign of finding the outer boundary of the city. At least ten separate building units with over 120 rooms have been excavated, many with multiple levels, and at least seven more buildings are known to be partly buried under the remaining ash. The site of Akrotiri runs along an old ravine today, its direction roughly north–south, and an ancient road axis (Telchines Road) links all the structures so far. Marinatos and Doumas divided the clusters of building units into mostly letter names, as Alpha, Beta, Gamma and Delta, as well as Xeste 1–4, West House and House of the Ladies. *Xeste*, named after a style of stone-walled buildings, comes from the Greek word for a dressed ashlar block of stone that fits together with others. This is the main type of construction found in these structures. To date, Akrotiri's largest excavated unit is Delta, with over forty rooms on several levels of four connected houses. The estimated population before the eruption is very difficult to reconstruct, but if even a conservative guess is made, it is likely that at least five thousand people lived in this city. This estimate is likely if its boundaries extend to about triple or quadruple its excavated area still under the unexcavated volcanic ash. Archaeologists can only guess at the rest of the island in Minoan antiquity, since so much of it was destroyed by the eruption and much still lies under volcanic ash. The archaeological excavations at Akrotiri show that it had considerable earthquake damage at about the same time the heavy volcanic ash fall buried the city, so these two phenomena are probably fairly simultaneous and connected.

The Akrotiri buildings are sophisticated, mostly stone-walled houses with well-planned doors and windows (framed by wooden beams) for ample light. Staircases rose to the upper floors, which were mostly residential areas. It is still astonishing that evidence can be found for plumbing in many of the rooms, along with the skilled use of water, especially in covered drains and even working toilets. It is no wonder that Thera has been called the Pompeii of the Aegean, because like that Roman city, its houses are so well preserved that Doumas could even pour plaster of paris into ash cavities to reconstruct furniture such as small tables. More exciting to some historians is the fact that Akrotiri was sealed by its volcanic destruction close to two thousand years before Pompeii. Thanks to the devastating volcano that sealed it off for almost 3,400 years, Akrotiri is by far the most complete city of the Aegean culture that we may ever know.

A personal tragedy for Marinatos—who continued working into his seventies—was that he suffered a massive stroke at the site of Akrotiri in 1974 and died almost immediately afterward. Christos Doumas capably continued the excavation and restoration work at Akrotiri from shortly after Marinatos's death in 1974 until 2001, when he officially retired from directing Akrotiri and teaching at the University of Athens. My wife and I were guests at Akrotiri for a week in 1998 with Christos and Alex Doumas, and their kind hospitality to other archaeologists like me is unforgettable. We lived in the House of the Muses on the site of Akrotiri as I pursued my own archaeological research. The gentle breezes from the sea filled our rooms, billowing our curtains and bringing the fragrance of the sea into our dreams at night just as they must have for the residents of Thera thousands of years ago.

The eruption destroyed the Minoan fleet on Crete and its ash spread to Palestine

Although many may have thought he was premature in 1939, Marinatos did not just jump to an irrational connection between Thera's eruption and a possible huge impact on Minoan civilization.

Archaeologists excavating on the larger island of Crete, seventy miles to the south, have discovered the port of Amnisos, the primary Minoan harbor on the north coast. Perhaps the most challenging artifacts to interpret turned out to be a destroyed fleet of ships, apparently smashed by a tidal wave that came from Thera itself at the time of eruption. Such a tidal wave would have accompanied massive underwater earthquakes, coalescing the waves into one giant tsunami that shattered the Minoan navy like matchsticks. This could have seriously compromised Minoan control of the Aegean Sea, a domination of the seas often called thalassocracy, with consequences in politics and commerce as well as military control. Such a conclusion would be an extension of what Marinatos thought back in 1939 but lacked supportive evidence to prove. Additional evidence of the cataclysm has also been found at Akrotiri, an event that must have resulted in some kind of possible Minoan naval collapse around the Aegean.

In Crete, Marinatos also excavated parts of the ancient port site of Amnisos and found a huge deposit of volcanic pumice there in the town. The Minoans fleeing Thera may have gathered pumice—an extremely light volcanic stone, filled with air bubbles—that rained from the sky, some of which would have floated awhile on the sea around the traces of Thera. Some scholars have recently suggested that the pumice was stored in ritual vessels on shrines at Amnisos, suggesting a religious fear or dread of the volcanic activity remembered from Thera. While the Thera eruption did not end Minoan civilization, it is likely to have been a contributing factor to eventual Minoan demise within a century.

The destruction of Thera must have been one of the most dramatic natural catastrophes in ancient history. Many scientists at various conferences about Thera have suggested that the power of the enormous volcanic explosion—caused in part by the pressure of boiling seawater, superheated and expanding, bursting through solid rock deep in the volcano's heart—would have exceeded that of a several-kiloton nuclear bomb. They suggest that this eruption's force would have been so loud that its sound would have been heard as far away as the Strait of Gibraltar to the west, as far south as central Africa and as far north as Scandinavia. The fallout—windblown ash covering hundreds of miles—has been well documented. The "shadow" of ash would have been deposited all across the eastern Mediterranean, including Anatolia (modern Turkey), as the high-altitude prevailing winds of the jet stream carried it eastward hundreds of miles. Eastern Crete was covered in places by ash layers several inches deep. Pumice washed up on the island of Anaphi fifteen miles away to a height of about forty feet, as high as a four-story building. The tidal wave would likely have reached the coast of Israel in little more than one and three-quarters of an hour and may have been around twenty feet high at that end point, judging by the pumice deposited there. This kind of seismic force, generated by underwater earthquakes accompanying the eruption, could have easily wiped out harbors and low coastal cities for hundreds of miles, indeed contributing to a temporary loss of maritime shipping and thoroughly disrupting an economy based on sea trade. So Marinatos was probably not far from the truth in theorizing that the Minoan civilization was partially brought to its knees by nature.

Akrotiri's preserved frescoes show the high level of art and civilization on Thera

Art is often an extension of a rich cultural life and an expression of wealth and leisure, but art is not so much a luxury as a creative outflow of a culture. Often, art expresses a culture's values in some way via visual information about life and religion. If we can reconstruct and read that art, in this case from a lost city, we may be able to grasp a deeper understanding of that culture.

Perhaps the most important discoveries at Akrotiri are the beautiful Minoan frescoes that covered many walls. Many of the houses of Akrotiri still have whole walls decorated floor to ceiling with colorful frescoes in the Minoan style, rich in nature and scenes of everyday life. Akrotiri has the highest concentration of surviving Minoan art because, much like Pompeii, it was completely buried in the ash fall of volcanic eruption and then immediately abandoned. Only since 1968 has this Minoan art reemerged to be appreciated again after 3,400 years. These frescoes of all hues include beautiful depictions of Minoan life, nearly all of which tell us how much the people of Thera loved nature.

West House, Room 5, contains several striking examples, including an exotic fantasy that may have been inspired by Egypt and the Nile, good evidence for trade with Egypt. Unusual animals, some mythical like griffins, chase each other along rivers where palm trees grow. In the nearby Fisherman fresco, a young man holds a bountiful catch of small tuna hanging from each hand. According to Doumas in 1983, the most important Akrotiri fresco is the Flotilla painting, also in this room, where a fleet of Minoan ships rows from one harbor to another. The ship details in this fresco tell us much about seafaring and ship construction of the Bronze Age. In Beta, Room 1, is a scene called Boxing Children, where boys with long plaits of black hair gracefully spar. On the diagonal wall in the same room is a scene of six antelopes, so freely and yet masterfully painted that they somehow appear both abstract and perfectly natural at the same time.

Blue monkeys cavort in a painting from Beta, Room 6, and these were first thought to have been imaginary animals until blue monkeys were reported from remote equatorial East Africa after the nineteenth century. This spectacular imagery suggests the surprising wealth of Thera, especially if it could show paintings of—or even import—such animals.

From Xeste 3, Room 3, one of the largest frescoes is still being painstakingly assembled out of thousands of tiny plaster chunks. This is the enigmatic and marvelous Saffron Gatherers, possibly depicting a goddess receiving adoration in offerings of saffron, long associated with spring and fertility. For several days I was able to watch the student conservators work for hours piecing together tiny plaster fragments. There were exultant shouts when they made perfect matches out of the bewildering array of seemingly never-ending pieces.

One masterpiece of ancient art that shows how close we are to the Therans is found in the area of Delta, Room 2. This is a perfectly preserved painting and one of the most beautiful, now known as the Spring fresco. The walls of this room are covered with clumps of lilies blooming from volcanic rock outcrops. Poised in the air over the flowers are Theran swallows, birds that today still dive and swoop along the island cliffs above the deep caldera far below. As the frescoed swallows circle each other with graceful wings over the blooming lilies, set against the sky, they appear to playfully dance in a bird courtship or mating ritual. Standing on the very edge of the cliff where blue sea engulfs the entire horizon, I have seen identical swallows dancing and diving along the dizzy heights, at the meeting of sea and sky almost close enough to reach and touch. One might immediately think of the myth of Daedalus and Icarus on Crete, yearning to fly and inspired to try from watching such birds. Clearly these Akrotiri wall paintings show that the people of Thera observed, revered and loved nature long before a violent natural disaster would ultimately destroy their city.

Rich trade with Egypt may have centered on valuable local items like emery

What was the source of wealth that made Akrotiri's art of such high quality? One easy answer is gathered from the evidence that Akrotiri and the Minoans at large had great trade contact with Egypt, to the mutual benefit of both cultures. Much of that evidence seems to come from the surviving art of Egypt, Crete and Thera. Egyptian elements are often seen in Akrotiri wall paintings, especially the Nile River scenes of West House, Room 5, where ducks and mallards appear to be directly copied from examples viewed in Egypt. Another possibility is that Minoan artists trained under Egyptian artists or that Egyptians also traveled to Akrotiri. Many Egyptian examples of traditional Nilotic scenes exist, such as those found a few centuries after Thera was destroyed in Nebamun's tomb paintings in Thebes.

Additionally, tomb paintings from Thebes in Egypt, especially from the Eighteenth Dynasty around 1550–1450 BC, also depict Minoan traders who crossed the sea to Egypt. Minoans painted in Rekhmire's and Senmut's tombs, for example, bring materials from Crete in vessels along with other items like bull heads, which both peoples' religions venerated. Not only are Minoans seen in Egypt but Egyptians are seen in Minoan art, for example, the Jewel Fresco of Minoan Knossos, with its person of "African" features wearing Egyptian-style jewelry. The Minoans were possibly known in Egypt as the Keftiu, which may be a reference to Crete and certainly refers to a people of the Aegean or eastern Mediterranean islands.

But what about the material evidence for trade—the actual artifact trade goods—between Egypt and Akrotiri or Minoan culture? What would the Aegeans have that Egypt wanted? This question is a little more complicated yet it relies less on interpretation than art does. Instead, we have texts, on what are called Linear A and B clay writing tablets, as well as the archaeological record to flesh out trade details. Unfortunately, while we can now read substantial Linear B tablets (Proto-Greek or Mycenean, mostly mainland texts), the script tablets of Linear A (Minoan or Cretan island texts) are still a muddle. Furthermore, no clay tablets of either Linear A or B script have been yet retrieved on Thera. But in this case, the exchange of actual trade can be confirmed through several different avenues including artifacts, but also found in ancient Egyptian vocabulary.

As mentioned, very ancient, predynastic (pre-3000 BC) Egyptian stone vessels made from diorite appeared in Crete in the Minoan Age (2100–1550 BC), if not before. Diorite is a hard stone that is very distinct and plentiful in Egypt but has not been found naturally to date in Cretan geological sources. Peter Warren and others have studied and published these vessels excavated from Minoan sites, which have been scientifically shown to be carved from Egyptian diorite.

On the other hand, there do not seem to be many commodities that the wealthy Egyptians would need from the Aegean. Certainly these early "Greek" commodities included olive oil and probably textiles, as Mycenaean archaeologist Cynthia Shelmerdine has convincingly shown. However—and this is a very provocative idea—there was a very valuable stone substance found only in the Aegean for which Egyptians would have a ready market but no local supply themselves. Perhaps this exotic stone not found in Egypt was all the more desirable because for thousands of years, Egypt's stone industries had been using very hard stone for sculpture, architecture, jewelry and amulets. Egyptians experimented with all kinds of technologies, always searching for the best materials to work with. This imported stone for which the Egyptians would have paid a premium was emery (scientifically known as corundum), and it was harder than anything else the Egyptians had for stone polishing. Second only to diamond on the Mohs scale of hardness, emery is rated as 9 to diamond's 10. Even quartzite and dolerite, the next hardest stoneworking tools in Egypt, are only about 7.5, and they are found naturally in Egypt's geology. Emery was then exclusively found on the Aegean island of Naxos, which was in close contact with Thera and possibly controlled by it. As I discovered on Thera in the artifact storage house at the site, the Bronze Age port of Moutsouna on eastern Naxos was shipping emery to elsewhere, including Akrotiri.

For years, Egyptologists have said that emery was not imported to Egypt until the Ptolemaic period (300–47 BC). This is when the word shows up in Ptolemaic Greek as *smeris* (the root word today for "emery"). But a few years ago I found the word *ysmerii* as an exotic imported stone in the Egyptian records of Pharaoh Thutmose III, circa 1450 BC, and that old argument about emery went out the window. This is still tentative, but here is a possible logical scenario: If Thera was a middleman "capital" Aegean island that controlled trade between Naxian emery and Egyptian markets—especially the royal stone workshops, which could afford this expensive and exotic stone, hardest in the ancient world—and if Theran culture had a monopoly on this stone and controlled this commodity of the Aegean trade (as in Plato's Atlantis), Egypt would have to pay a high price for it. Emery would assist the Egyptians in making their countless hard stone sculptures; and only emery gave Egyptian masons the means to achieve a polish on hard stone sculpture like granite or quartzite, a polish that no other stone material could bring. Is this one possible reason why the people of Thera could afford such a high standard of art and civilization?

The destruction of Thera helps to date the end of the Middle Bronze Age

There is still deep controversy today among historians and archaeologists about both the chronology and the reasons why the Middle Bronze Age ended in the Mediterranean. The date offered for years in textbooks as the vague end of the Middle Minoan (around the Middle Bronze Age) and the beginning of the Late Bronze Age has been 1550 BC. Trying to match this date to an abrupt end of the Middle Kingdom and the beginning of the New Kingdom in Egyptian dynasties has been very tricky, and Egyptian history calls this the Second Intermediate Period, between 1700 and 1550 BC. But the newly accepted early date of Thera's destruction, around 1620 BC, falls exactly in the middle between these dates, equidistant between the ambiguous end of the Middle Bronze Age and the beginning of the Late Bronze Age, which some place now around 1700 BC.

If the destruction of Thera around 1620 BC is in any way applicable here, it might provide the when and possibly the why about how these ancient cultures began to change so radically. This is especially true in the Aegean world, because it dovetails nicely with these dual Egyptian and Mediterranean/Minoan histories as we understand them. Furthermore, rather than contradict, it better explains the noticed change in material cultures. At this time nobody else—especially the Egyptians—ventured out into the open seas or had the knowledge to do so. So when the tidal wave from Thera's destruction crushed many of their ships, along with their navigating mariners in their island harbors, the Minoans of Crete and Akrotiri obviously lost a considerable portion of their maritime advantage. If this hypothesis is right, the Aegean islands also lost their monopolies on certain materials, and the major trade routes commanded by Minoans between Egypt, Palestine and the Aegean were affected for generations. Although connecting the chronology is hugely problematic, the historian J. G. Bennett has even tried to associate Thera's destruction and the darkness brought by its spreading volcanic ash over the eastern Mediterranean with the biblical plagues of Egypt described in the book of Exodus. N. Platon, the great Greek archaeologist working on Crete, also wondered a few decades ago whether certain Egyptian texts, such as this one, refer to the influence of Thera:

> The sun is covered and does not shine to the sight of men. Life is no longer possible when the sun is concealed behind the clouds. Ra has turned his face from mankind.

In stable Egypt along the usually predictable Nile to the deep south, thick airborne ash from Thera's eruption could have greatly diminished the sunlight so needed for life and agriculture, and this could have been temporarily catastrophic as well. It may yet happen that archaeologists and historians will all agree that the Mycenaeans from mainland Greece, successors to the island culture Minoans, eventually picked up the pieces of the Aegean trade and ruled the fragments of the Minoan world when they carefully ventured out again into the sea. These trading peoples would have been followed by the Phoenicians, who became the next wave of great mariners of the ancient world, not intimidated by open water and eager to ply their commerce beyond the shining water of the horizon.

Conclusion

Plato may have been only trying to cobble different versions of old myths together, and Atlantis may not ever be proven to be Thera, but such a connection is certainly worthy of continuing research scholarship. Gauged by Akrotiri alone, the wealth of the island of Thera is not as surprising as was once thought, especially if it was such an important Minoan entrepôt before the volcanic eruption "sank" the island. Connecting its multistoried town, its lovely frescoes and the likely trade in emery from other islands under its hegemony, Akrotiri and Thera make more sense now than ever before.

After years of waiting to prove his ideas while looking closely at the land around him, Marinatos's first exciting field day in 1967 proved the discovery of Akrotiri was no accident. When Marinatos first dug at Akrotiri, standing in the fine ash blown by the wind across the island in the middle of the blue sea, he must have wondered how he would be remembered. But Marinatos was a patient man. Thinking about the long, slow years that had passed between his ideas being ridiculed in 1939 when he was laughed at, and this day in 1967 when the beautiful clay vessels began to emerge from the volcanic ash under his feet, Marinatos had the last laugh. After all, he could have smiled to himself, Akrotiri had waited millennia under the ash, so why shouldn't he have waited a few decades to answer his own question?

Chapter 9

Olduvai Gorge
The Key to Human Evolution

Olduvai Gorge, East Africa, 1959

Louis and Mary Leakey had been eking out an
austere existence in East Africa for decades
without much attention or success, living almost
hand-to-mouth on small grants while they looked
painstakingly for the earliest human ancestors. If
they hadn't been so dedicated, they would have
given up years before.

But everything changed on July 17, 1959. Mary
Leakey was working solo because Louis was sick.
She was accompanied on a promising new survey
walk by a local cameraman, Des Bartlett, who
produced British safari films but had expressed interest in filming an excavation just for the novelty.
They were walking at Olduvai near the junction of
two gorges, a depression bed called a *korongo* in the
local African dialect, rich in bones and stone artifacts. On foot Mary and Des explored an unexcavated site the Leakeys had named FLK. Recent
rains had washed soil and dust away, freshly expos-
ing embedded objects and removing surface dust

and soil. Archaeologists like Mary Leakey learn fast from experience how rains can make artifacts stand out sharply on the surface, including here on the mixed basalt-limestone of FLK. Sharp-eyed Mary was looking at the ground as she walked along the edge of the eroded *korongo* bed when something caught her attention. This was a thick mastoid skull fragment sticking up like new from the old soil surface that had almost certainly just been cleaned by the rain. Mary immediately noticed the teeth were hominid and not those of another primate, and that a lot of the skull was apparently embedded there. It was the find of her career.

Mary ran back breathlessly to Louis in camp, who jumped out of his bed despite being ill, and they rushed together to FLK and began carefully excavating the hominid skull, all the while being captured in film segments on the spot by Des Bartlett. Thus, the exact process of finding and excavating this discovery was memorialized in film. Although Louis was a bit disappointed, probably because he was hoping for a later homo artifact and possibly because Mary found it instead of him, he promptly named its genus as *Zinjanthropus* after an Arabic word (*zinj*) for "East Africa" combined with "man" (*anthropus*). The species name was given in honor of Charles Boise, one of the Leakeys' few sponsors. Soon after, when shown to a curious and receptive crowd at the African archaeology section of the Pan-African Congress, *Zinjanthropus boisei* also came to light as a television and media star. No one could dispute the validity of their excavation— caught on film from its very moment of discovery—and news of *Zinjanthropus* was soon published in the preeminent international science journal *Nature* as a major australopithecine discovery.

The film media—sensing a new role after having captured this discovery—soon realized themselves how important documentary films could be. They had tremendous appeal to a science-hungry world, which could now witness discoveries up close by film. Louis Leakey, knowing a lucky circumstance had changed their lives, wisely capitalized on this media prospect more than anyone else at the time. The area where the skull was found was later proved by a new potassium-argon (K-Ar) dating method to go back 1.7 million years, and this one fossil paleontology find brought the Leakeys science celebrity status and much-needed funding from the National Geographic Society. This vaulted the Leakey name into the academic limelight and guaranteed their continuing work, including Louis's later *Homo habilis* find. But as Brian Fagan acknowledges in his *Oxford Companion to Archaeology* (1996), "The discovery of *Zinjanthropus boisei* was a turning point in the study of human origins."

Out of Africa

"Out of Africa" is not just a theoretical phrase about something so distant it doesn't matter, nor is it a romantic notion embedded in a movie title. If you ask the average person on the street what the phrase "out of Africa" means, you might hear a range of answers, some incorrect, but many people will know it refers to human origins. Here are a few reasons why the discovery of human ancestors in and around Olduvai Gorge lying in the Great Rift of Africa changed history permanently.

Important questions about human origins were answered at Olduvai, and continuing research has only confirmed this. Due to geology and plate tectonics, the African Great Rift Zone is an ideal place for sleuthing human origins. Growing up nearby, Louis Leakey and later his family were well suited as pioneers to search for human ancestors in Africa; in fact, the Leakeys are often referred to as the "First Family of Human Origins." As seen above, the Leakeys' discovery of *Zinjanthropus* (now called *Paran-thropus boisei*) in 1959 electrified the world and turned global attention to Africa. Following the Leakeys, in 1974 Donald Johanson found "Lucy," and proved she belonged to the australo-pithecine branch of the early "human" family.

This complex story cannot be easily told from its earliest stages, but we can pick it up as it was articulated and became a quest over the last few centuries, finally coming to fruition in the early and mid twentieth century. The story of the fairly recent discovery of human origins is as exciting as any other discovery in our history.

A deep gorge splits East Africa, hundreds of feet deep in some places, mostly shallower in others. One section of it is named Olduvai. You can see across the gorge where the rocks have been gradually pulled apart by geological forces over millions of years, a tumble of loose talus marking its old eroded edges. This divergent continental plate boundary divides the tectonic units of Africa in an invisibly slow process of separation. Perhaps a few million years ago the split was not as wide, and at that time our earliest tool-making ancestors lived, hunted or searched for sources of the perfect stone along the gorge for hundreds of miles. Sometimes they were not the hunters but the hunted, caught and torn piecemeal by ravenous saber-toothed tigers and other huge beasts that were probably far more fierce than the big cat and hyena descendants now living in the natural parks and preserves of Africa. When these hominid ancestors' bones were buried or scattered in this rift valley, time reabsorbed some of the bones and either fossilized them or embedded them in more recent lime-stone rock, like cement made up from old lake bed sediments, powdery stuff that water soon turned into a natural concrete.

Because Olduvai Gorge, like East Africa around it, was also a volcanic region, later lava flows even poured across the same fissured surfaces, often covering the fossilized bones under deepening layers. Some of these bones had already turned into silica copies of their original shapes. If we can imagine what these primeval hunters looked like, it may be difficult to picture them as recognizably human. They usually had longer arms with denser bones and their hip and knee joints were not as fully adapted to being upright, although their speed in flight must have still been phenomenally fast. If not fully covered with hair, nature nonetheless offered them more protection than modern humans have. Some aspects would have already begun to separate them from other primates; their crania were shaped very differently from chimpanzees' and gorillas', with much larger forebrains protected by less prominent brows. But it was the eyes in their erect heads that would have glinted with more than a glimmer of intelligence: they knew they had to survive against formidable and far stronger enemies. This incentive for adaptation to their circumstances brought out capacities for finding better weapons and tools beyond their own hands. They knew from growing experience that a stone in their hands was stronger and more durable than their own flesh, a tougher extension of themselves. Such stones held in their hands offered the power to withstand their natural enemies and enabled them to utilize the resources around them: their hands could not break wood or rock, but a strong stone in their hands, even slightly broken and altered to a sharper edge, would cut wood and other harder substances with which their world was filled, making life a little less harsh. They feared and respected fire, like the wild animals around them, but at some point they began to see fire as an ally, standing near where the savannahs burned from lightning strikes, inching ever closer in curiosity through the millennia to that magical moment when they could capture fire and use it without being burned. Somewhere along this gradual, slow continuum, these primates became what we would agree was truly human.

Why questions about human origins are important

Some people would subvert the question of human origins into a religious debate, often out of fear of complexity or the unknown. Having to really seek new answers instead of swallow old dogma can be harder for certain minds to accept. But understanding who we are and how we developed or evolved is part of our deeper human experience. In reality, we are probably not fully human if we do not reflect on this question, because to be fully human means to constantly and intelligently search for answers to difficult questions. This complex question is confounding because its possible answers derive from the oldest possible time imaginable, an inquiry so much earlier than most others we could ask, especially since we have no legible history of events so long ago.

Alternate views of the cosmos and our place in it have always been around, despite what religion says. From the dawn of time not everyone has been so easily persuaded that the shamans, priests and oracles knew all the answers they claimed. The scientific revolutions of the Renaissance and the following Enlightenment showed it was not only acceptable but necessary to seek more information about human history and prehistory.

Copernican proof in the sixteenth century—probably laid out by Aristarchus of Samos in the third century BC and later suppressed or forgotten—transformed perceptions about the earth's true place in the solar system and brought a new humility to astronomy, which some found frightening. Geology and other sciences followed with radical interpretations about history, among them the ideas that the universe and earth were far older than the supposed moment of creation in 4004 BC. But the most radical idea of time past to come from the beginnings of modern science was that the human species wasn't created but in fact evolved and could possibly even be shown in transitional stages. Adam and Eve were no longer a single pair of individuals but a generic set of the first genetic parents who might not easily resemble us, their latest offspring.

Charles Darwin, who had considered a career in theology after Cambridge, hypothesized around 1871 in *The Descent of Man and Selection in Relation to Sex* that Africa might be the source of the human family. As Ann Gibbons tells it now (2006):

> Darwin chose Africa because humans' closest cousins in the animal kingdom—chimpanzees and gorillas—lived in Africa; therefore, he wrote, "it is more probable that our early progenitors lived on the African continent than elsewhere." But Darwin admitted that it was "useless to speculate on this subject," since an extinct European ape nearly as large as humans could also have given rise to humans.

The Darwinian idea of descent from related primates has had enough well-known and widely published impact on conservative thinking to not need any amplification here, but what made Olduvai so incredibly important is that it brought much-needed evidence to the search for the missing links in primate evolution.

A Dutch doctor and anatomist, Eugene Dubois (1858–1940), looked for missing links in Asia and found the incomplete bone remains of what is popularly called Java Man in 1891 in Indonesia. He named his find *Pithecanthropus erectus* but it now belongs to the category of *Homo erectus*. Dubois was vilified from many directions and is still attacked by antievolutionists claiming he faked and then later recanted his evidence, which is both terribly unfair and untrue. This is the price he paid for being the first to substantiate Darwin with early human finds.

But before Louis Leakey (1903–72), only Raymond Dart and a few others made Africa the focus of early human research, as paleontologists of the time would rarely venture to Africa to look for the kind of evidence needed. Raymond Dart (1893–1988) was the noted physical anthropologist and anatomist who had already found australopithecine skeletal remains in South Africa in 1924, in the famous fossilized Taung baby skull embedded in limestone. Dart's controversial claim to finding this new fossil human ancestor, which he named *Australopithecus africanus* ("Southern African ape-man") was not well received by the global scientific community, let alone Darwin's detractors in the religious world. Dart's startling find was variously called a fluke, an anomalous accident or just a misinterpretation of the fossil remains. His paleontologist colleague from Scotland, Robert Broom, was one of the few who stood against the tide of criticism and joined Dart in South Africa, finding more fragmentary fossil australopithecine remains, although they worked in relative obscurity for decades. Knowledgeable in dentistry, Dart had pointed out the difference in teeth between other primates and early hominids: early hominids lacked the frightening fangs of their primate cousins, with smaller incisors and molars for grinding. Part of this was dietary and part was adaptation to dependence on stone tools that would do the work of fangs, just as Darwin had theorized. Thus, both lower jaws and mastoidal skull fragments with reliable dentation were believed by Dart and Broom to be tremendously important. But more evidence was needed to flesh out Darwin's theories, and while Africa was believed by many evolutionary pioneers to be the place, the locations and details of human origins were only just beginning to be connected from general theory to specific credible paleontological fieldwork.

The African Great Rift Zone is an ideal place for sleuthing

Darwin made one of the first stabs in the near dark about related geological masses across continents. Plate tectonics is a given in today's accepted canon of earth science, but Darwin's query was almost a century before continental drift and plate tectonics were formally postulated. Darwin's observations in South Africa and South America foreshadowed Louis Leakey's later hunch about human origins in Africa by at least a half century.

As mentioned, the geology of the Great Rift, like nearly any plate tectonic boundary, was active and divergent, caused by the spreading of the continents of Asia and Africa away from each other. Almost always accompanied by volcanism on one or both sides, like the "Ring of Fire" on the Pacific Ocean's plate margins, such rift zones penetrate deep into the earth's thin crust. East Africa's Olduvai Gorge is such a place, a remnant of long geological change over scores of millions of years. This rift is marked by several phenomena, one of which is that a plate boundary slowly breaks up and gradually exposes on its edges the much deeper buried sediments and layers that would not otherwise be so visible, except in such active rift zones. Thus, fossils can turn up at a much higher density in a rift zone such as Olduvai Gorge. Another phenomenon is possibly more important for early human ancestry: the geology at a rift zone frequently includes obsidian, and all hominids and later humans would seek out toolmaking stone like obsidian or basalt because of related volcanic activity. Obsidian is the stone of choice for cutting, for weapons and for many other tool needs because, as volcanic glass, it fractures conchoidally very much like man-made glass, being nearly the sharpest cutting material in nature. Wherever obsidian can be found, it is always a high-value commodity. Abundance of obsidian is likely one of the things attracting early hominids to this location, as well as the fact that water also collected here in low points across the gorge's terrain, drawing the animals that were hunted for food and the food chain's predatory beasts as well.

To underestimate the earliest hominids by not appreciating their experimental and experiential awareness of stone would be a grave mistake. That a young Louis Leakey noted all the numerous obsidian stone fragments embedded in the low cliffs of this part of the African rift valley was very prescient. But Leakey was also likely to have made the other associations with long-term plentiful water and animal life because he had grown up alongside these very watering holes in this very rift valley.

Louis Leakey was well suited to search for human ancestors in Africa

In her 1995 biography of Louis Leakey, *Ancestral Passions*, Virginia Morell has documented Leakey's early childhood and youth in East Africa. Born to British missionary parents living in the Kikuyu tribal territory, Louis was incredibly familiar with the land from having played and rambled across it since childhood. His first boyhood find of fossils made an indelible impression on him and began a lifelong passion for natural science and ultimately paleontology, the search for early life.

Louis Leakey would have most likely been puzzled as a youth about both the commonalities and wide differences between his own missionary family, British expatriates, and the Kikuyu tribe into which he was initiated like his playmates. He would have heard the biblical stories about Adam and Eve from his Christian parents in their mission environment but could not have failed to ponder—perhaps more than most people of his generation because of his circumstances—how much humanity had widely diverged over millennia from a supposedly common parentage.

Africa was a natural living classroom and intellectual laboratory for young Leakey. This early reflection of human diversity and the colorful complexity of tribal and clan relationships, with so many intricate behavioral codes and necessary taboos, compared to the cultural template of British expatriate life, must have naturally drawn him to anthropology as a university student at Cambridge. He already knew more experientially about Africa than his classmates and probably more than many of his professors. His African upbringing would also have made him much more comfortable in Africa among fellow hybridized expatriates than among the reserved British society, as so often happens to children of missionaries when they travel. For missionary children, "abroad" does not usually mean their adopted homeland but the original country of their parents. So after distinguishing himself at Cambridge in one of the world's most rigorous programs, where Darwin's challenging work was seen as brilliant theory needing verification, Leakey naturally returned to Africa where his immediate roots lay. There, Leakey was able to add more flesh to theory and coalesce his new intellectual discipline with life experiences. Of course, Louis Leakey commented ironically in 1966 on opposition to his search for human ancestors in Africa: "I was told as a young student not to waste my time searching for Early Man in Africa, since everyone knew he had started in Asia" (quoted in Ann Gibbons, *The First Human*, 2006).

As early as 1929, after Cambridge and back in the native Africa he knew so well from childhood, the twenty-six-year-old Leakey had seen a high density of what he thought looked like stone tools at Kariandusi, Kenya. This assortment of stone included enough flaked black obsidian and related volcanic tool fragments littering the area to seriously merit beginning his search at Kariandusi. Such obsidian or volcanic glass would have been the optimum material for stone tools then as now.

Leakey's ultimate graduate education, a doctorate in paleontology, only built upon what he had observed from childhood about Africa while living in Kenya and Tanzania. Thus, Louis Leakey was one of the most perfectly suited individuals in history to search for human ancestors in the East Africa of his birth, living in a land where his earliest childhood explorations had trained his keen eyes to see what others had missed: an incredibly long prehistory of human life. Where others only saw endless rocks in dry riverbeds, Louis Leakey saw artifacts.

Louis had married his second wife, Mary Nicol, after she had joined him as an artist to draw his finds in the field, although this led to a divorce from his first wife Frida and a tarnished social reputation. Mary Leakey was actually a better archaeologist/ paleontologist than Louis—she was more disciplined and careful with the material evidence and the tedious work of excavation, thus providing the needed rigorous scientific verifiability. Although she would always credit Louis for being the visionary teacher, as mentioned, it was Mary who first made the well-publicized discovery of *Zinjanthropus*, the australopithecine proof that validated Darwin and magnetized the world's attention to their joint research.

By the 1950s Louis and Mary Leakey, still working under the difficult circumstances of little funding, as they had since the 1930s, began to concentrate their human ancestor search efforts in the ancient lake beds torn apart by the continental divergent plate boundary of the Great Rift Valley at Olduvai. Mary Leakey had already found a new *Proconsul* primate fossil a few years earlier that brought them some attention but not enough to generate adequate funds for full-scale fieldwork. While Mary's find riveted the scientific world, it would not have been possible without Louis Leakey's unshakable confidence that this search for human origins was their lifework and would ultimately bear fruit. Louis also had a keen awareness of the huge public curiosity about human origins and an ability to inspire others to seek out their own path in this pursuit. Following Mary Leakey's discovery of *Zinjanthropus* in 1959 and the National Geographic Society's sponsorship of their research, Louis and Mary Leakey were ultimately lionized for their dedication and vision over many decades, proving with hard science what had previously been only theoretical.

The Leakeys: First Family of Human Origins

For over seventy-five years now the Leakeys have been acknowledged as the "First Family of Human Origins." Because of the Leakeys, paleontology and paleoanthropology became respected fields and attracted legions of students who themselves later became pioneers in related academic careers as new finds grew exponentially. From the early 1960s onward, Louis Leakey concentrated more and more on public speaking, publicity and fund-raising ventures that promoted new research. In fieldwork,

Louis and Mary complemented each other. Louis was restlessly impetuous, always looking for the larger picture, where Mary was more cautious and extremely diligent about detail. But the visionary and enthusiastic Louis also started the careers of several of his promising interns like Jane Goodall, noted chimpanzee primatologist, and Dian Fossey, equally devoted to studies of gorillas. The Leakey children, raised on archaeology sites and ultimately making their own important finds, included Jonathan and then Richard, who had great results in the Lake Turkana rift zone sites and made significant *Homo erectus* (*Homo ergaster*) finds. Richard eventually left archaeology and paleontology to champion animal preservation, but his wife, Meave, continued the Leakey legacy with further decades of African fieldwork. Now some of Richard and Meave's children, including Louise Leakey, who works with her mother, maintain the family preeminence in human origins, with new hominid finds that stretch the dates even further back. To claim that the Leakeys have done more than anyone else in the field is unfair, but their almost dynastic visibility has certainly changed world perceptions for the better as more and more have accepted human evolution. The name Leakey will be forever associated with early human research.

Donald Johanson proved Lucy belonged to the australopithecines

Other paleontology pioneers followed in the Leakeys' footsteps at Olduvai, Laetoli, Koobi Fora and many other African Great Rift sites. Now-famous names like Donald Johanson, Tim White and Nicolas Toth have joined the ranks with spectacular early human and early stone technology finds as well as continuing primate studies that demonstrate startling primate relationships.

On November 30, 1974, Donald Johanson made perhaps one of the most dramatic paleoanthropology finds ever. Johanson, who had visited the aging Louis Leakey in 1970, was working far to the north in the same Great Rift Zone in the Afar region of northeast Ethiopia with biological anthropologist Tim White and others. In the remote Hadar Desert, rich in fossil deposits, Johanson discovered a complete fragmentary fossil skeleton in a spot that his team had prosaically called Locality 162 in numeric shorthand. Because it was a complete fossil skeleton—a first—and could be determined to be female, it was an incredibly huge find, riveting the world's attention because people could identify with it in a more personal way. This female skeleton, originally marked as Hadar specimen AL 288-1, would be affectionately named "Lucy"; and as her species, *Australopithecus afarensis*, was then acknowledged as the earliest hominid, she was thus—at 3.2 to 3.5 million years—much older than the Leakeys' previous australopithecines.

In 1994, the field of paleoanthropology was stretched to new limits by Tim White's discovery of *Australopithecus ramidus*. This find was datable to 3.8 million years, not long after the first human ancestors separated from the other primates in an event that is difficult to reconstruct because, as expected, the artifactual links become fewer and farther apart the deeper we go back in unrecorded time.

Conclusion

The Leakeys took Darwin's unproven ideas seriously and brought the needed evidence for human evolution to light in a public way that remains seminal to this day. We should always be ready to encourage new people like the Leakeys who are not content with the intellectual status quo. Pioneers are less likely to sit still and more likely to explore in directions that may be uncomfortable to many. Pioneers in discovery don't come cheaply—they need solid education and training, otherwise they might not come at all. Major discoveries like those the Leakeys made are often returns on intellectual investments made by previous generations.

Even with accidental discoveries, usually someone recognizes the importance, in even the minutest evidence, of what others would ignore. While it may take years for momentum to build, with evidence strong enough to persuade those who know what to look for and where to look (rare qualities few of us possess), new discoveries will eventually lead to whole new vistas on the burgeoning landscape of knowledge. Recent discoveries will themselves be catalysts to future discoveries, and then to exciting chapters yet unwritten for understanding human prehistory and history. We are, after all, the inheritors of those earliest humans who reached into the African riverbeds with new curiosity. They stretched out their hands and wrapped them around a stone in a moment that altered both the hands and the mind and perhaps even imperceptibly the stone itself forever, making it no longer just a stone, but a tool.

Other members of the Leakey family, Meave and Louise specifically, may now have found the oldest human ancestor yet, cautiously dated around 4 million years old. Additional recent australopithecine finds (in Dikika, Ethiopia, also in the Afar region where Lucy is from) include, in 2000, a new female infant skeleton now called "Lucy's daughter" although she may be one hundred thousand years older than Lucy. Still, this is quite an age for Lucy, who, if she was anything like one of her possible descendants millions of years later, would not be so glib about revealing her age or date of birth.

Chapter 10

Tomb of 10,000 Warriors
The Key to Imperial China

China, 1974

It was a cold early spring day in central China and a slight ground mist hovered, making Lishan Hill look as if it were floating over a thin white sea. A small group of farmers, pooling their labor, peered from under their broad Shensi hats in the frosty air as they looked carefully over the freshly plowed earth for the best spot to dig a well. Trying to find where the sinking water table was closest to the surface seemed risky, but they needed more water for the crops they planned to put in. The spring rains had not come with nearly enough water and even the normally muddy river was low and sluggish. The spring of 1974 was another relentlessly dry year, disastrous for fulfilling the quotas the bureaucrats had set for them far away in Beijing, the farmers grumbled.

They dug with shovels and picks through the resisting clay, knowing their backs would be sore at the end of the exhausting day. Their depth slowly increased; at first they were at their knees, then their waists and finally by sundown at the end of the first day, their shoulders. They would have to go even deeper to find the water table. The second day was a little easier as the clay became moister as they dug. They descended below the surface so that even their straw hats were below the feet of the supervisor, whose barking voice directed them from above. Then, about thirteen feet from the surface, first one and then a second farmer stopped as both a pick and a shovel almost simultaneously struck something harder and more unyielding than the clay. Their blades rang with a harsh clanging sound. At about the same time, two other farmers hit a hole that gaped open beneath them. These two events caught everyone's attention and the supervising boss walked up to the very edge of the trench to take a closer look at what had stopped the work. He ordered them to dig around this protruding clay-covered object to lift whatever it was out of the way so they could continue. He also ordered another farmer to go back to the village for a flashlight, torch or some kind of light to explore the deep hole because its bottom could not be seen.

One farmer removed powdery clay from around the top of the exposed object, and the others dug deeper around it, but as they cleared the clay, they were surprised and a little frightened to note it was a human head attached to shoulders and more body beneath that. The farmers were superstitious, but the supervisor assured them that it wasn't real, however lifelike it appeared—that it was only a statue. The supervisor was now irritated at the delay, but he ordered two farmers to extract the statue, if that was what it was, and ordered the others to continue digging. But soon they struck other huge lifelike ceramic figures wherever they dug. When a light was brought, the same fallen rows of terra-cotta figures turned up in the hollow dark gallery beneath them.

The supervisor began to be alarmed, but, despite the slowing and even temporary stoppage of their important well-digging job, his curiosity was soon aroused. Perhaps there was a treasure here. He wondered how soon he would have to notify his own bosses and explain the delay to the authorities. By the end of the day, however, even with farmers from other villages helping to dig, no treasure was found, even in the underground gallery. More of these endless terra-cotta human figures stretched in every direction they explored. These lifeless but imposing figures were taller than all of them by almost a foot. Some figures were still standing, but most were on their sides or backs or leaning into each other. As they cleaned the emerging statues a bit throughout the day, these rural farmers could see that all these figures were dressed as soldiers from long ago.

The supervisor was disappointed but notified the authorities the next morning of a delay in the well-digging work. His bosses came and saw for themselves the many ceramic soldiers dressed in ancient costumes. They noted the farmers would have to dig their well elsewhere in the plain until this could be resolved. Finally, proper archaeological authorities were brought all the way from Beijing. These archaeologists and bureaucrats could hardly restrain their excitement when they saw the ceramic soldiers; they took notes about the clothing and, based on this detail, dated the ceramic figures to just before the Han dynasty, well over two thousand years ago. The farmers who first struck the figures with their tools or exposed the underground gallery came back as often as they could between days of well digging elsewhere, both curious and proud, while they still had access to the site. The archaeologists slowly marked off the abandoned well-digging site and after a proper survey, began to excavate this anonymous field below Lishan Hill. This site would forever alter perceptions about ancient China and how its imperial age began. It was soon called the Tomb of 10,000 Warriors because of its apparently endless rows of terra-cotta statues. Even the archaeologists who first dug here at Lishan cannot confirm this exact story.

As mentioned, some of the world's greatest archaeological discoveries in modern history were accidents, not found by professionals searching years for a known object or monument, but instead by complete amateurs who likely had no idea of the importance of their finds when they chanced upon them. It is probable that most of the accidental discoverers would never know how much their discoveries would impact the flow of history beyond their own lifetimes.

How important is this discovery and what circumstances prove its history-making impact? This site, near the ancient city of Xi'an, has the largest mausoleum and the greatest single tomb artifact assemblage in the world, with almost uncountable surviving artifacts. Partly because of how the tomb was constructed, the objects within are in excellent condition. This tomb shows examples of early Chinese technology—especially intense metallurgy—at an earlier stage than known before, and it even provides details not previously known, such as examples of some martial arts at an early historical stage. The thousands of clay or terra-cotta warriors are amazingly detailed with individual features, seeming to represent traditions of ten different Chinese ethnic groups as well as giving a true sense of a unifying empire. The Qin dynasty emperor who created this marvel also imposed a drastic and rigid restructuring onto Chinese society. The tomb helps us understand why the Han dynasty—with its great flowering of Chinese culture—followed the Qin dynasty's first unification of China. Because of its vastness and the amazing details of its artifacts, this site has stimulated archaeology in China more than any other site.

Local geography of China and historical background of "the first true emperor"

China has a long history that dates back to the beginning of rice cultivation and the last stone tools of the Neolithic Age more than eight thousand years ago. Myth shrouds much of the early history of China. The first emperor was said to be Huangdi of the Shang dynasty somewhere around 2000–1800 BC in Western chronology, but before this discovery there was no compelling evidence for real imperial control of China's vast territory before the Han dynasty around 200 BC, when warring clans were brought together to make China one nation.

Looking at a map of Asia shows clearly how China developed independently from the rest of Asia and the West. Geography offers credible evidence for the isolation of one culture from another, with natural barriers that allow only a trickle of change over millennia. China is set off on the north by deserts like the Gobi of Mongolia and in the east and south by seas around the Pacific Ocean. On its western edge, China has a wall of enormous mountain chains, including the Himalayas, hundreds of snow-glistening peaks, some reaching well over twenty-five thousand feet, and the Tibetan High Plateau, at an average of ten thousand feet, itself higher than many major mountain chains in the world. No wonder China has been unknown to the West for much of history, an exotic land where abundant mystery was kept secret by isolation.

To the east of these mountains, in China itself, great rivers flow west from the high ranges through many hills and along broadening valleys. Both the Yangtze and the Yellow River have been used as highways and conduits of human traffic for thousands of years. It is no accident that the Tomb of 10,000 Warriors—at Lintong near Xi'an in Shaanxi Province—is roughly in the center of ancient China between the two great communication chains of these rivers, since these waterways and control of them were vital to ruling China's broad lands. Xi'an's optimum location offered China's first real emperor an opportunity to connect many regions into one land that would be an empire. Now the Xi'an area is home to the most important archaeological site in China. The site, actually about twenty-seven miles from Xi'an and adjacent to the Wei River, is called the Tomb of 10,000 Warriors, although this is a poetic exaggeration because there are actually only somewhere between seven and eight thousand warrior statues. "The first true emperor" of China wanted to make an unforgettable impression on his own people and on future generations.

Although not everyone agrees with some of these details, the owner of the great tomb was Zheng Qin (259–210 BC) and he began ruling at age thirteen around 246 BC. He was the first leader to unify China into an empire, forcibly connecting six different antagonistic states. This first real emperor's name has several variations. Although in early life he was Zheng Qin (Zheng is also often spelled Xeng), or the "Tiger of Qin," he is mostly later known as Qin Shihuangdi or just Shihuangdi. *Huangdi* can also be a generic word for "emperor," styled after the name of the first mythical Shang dynasty ruler. Qin Shihuangdi ruled for about thirty-six years from 246 BC to when he was about fifty years old in 210 BC, and started the Qin (or Chi'in) dynasty, from which China's name was probably first derived. From inscriptions at this site and others, Qin Shihuangdi appears to have been both very canny and ruthless as well as politically well advised, making many changes to Chinese society with autocratic laws. Most of these harsh new laws were completely necessary to form a centralized government and make his empire possible.

Thanks greatly to this immense tomb, historians can now make sense of China's early imperial history and how this first empire was achieved. Some of Qin Shihuangdi's decrees have been preserved and they show exactly how his sweeping changes were enacted. He surrounded himself with wise, capable scholars and canny administrators who offered effective advice on how to proceed with building an empire. Unifying China would not have been possible without much of the drastic and previously unthinkable changes Qin Shihuangdi enforced on the people. At least eighty thousand households were uprooted or even destroyed to achieve his ends.

The emperor Qin Shihuangdi first suppressed and then eliminated dissent, especially from the many Confucian scholars who pursued individualism. Most of the Confucian scholars were simply killed and others banished, and their books were burned to suppress their dangerous ideas about individualism. His ruthless ways—such as decreeing mass murder and destroying whole villages as well as anyone who displeased him—were cruel and unnecessary, and he became (or already was) a megalomaniac. What little education was permitted soon became just yet another method to force thought and philosophy only along certain pathways. Obedience to authority became a highly encouraged and rewarded virtue. Here is one very telling decree inscribed on a bronze tablet from 221 BC:

In the 26th year [of Qin Shihuangdi's reign], all the feudal states were merged by his majesty. Civilians are now in peace, the Huangdi title is claimed for the emperor's great achievements. The ministers Zhuang and Wan are thus instructed to standardize and unify the measurements which cause confusion.

Standardizing all the laws and bureaucratic administration was one way to achieve the emperor's central power, but even the

Chinese writing system and measurements, including currency and weights, were changed throughout the land of China. Besides the obvious propaganda of why Qin Shihuangdi deserved the title of emperor—bestowing "peace on civilians"—we note from this decree how his ministers Zhuang and Wan assist the centralization. They removed the "confusion" that accompanied the variations in different regional sets of weights and measurements over hundreds of miles. Since China had many regions and dialects, traditional symbols and old ways of counting would have been obstacles to unification. But administering such an empire also had another goal. This was to eliminate "confusion" for bureaucrats who had to implement imperial census and taxation. Taxation, one of the single most important resources for an empire, had to derive from good records. Careful census based on detailed economic assessments needed to be made uniform before such taxes could be collected. Thus, if the empire were to succeed, economic confusion could not be tolerated. Emperor Qin Shihuangdi could achieve even greater power if one set of quantifying and linguistic tools were used throughout the old "Warring States" of China. Such massive changes would have been painful and not without resistance, but the new Qin dynasty brutally achieved this goal under the first real emperor, Qin Shihuangdi. His vast tomb underscores that power in ways never seen before and perhaps never again after his death in 210 BC.

The Xi'an site has the largest mausoleum in the world

The entire mausoleum site covers over twenty-one square miles, almost half the size of San Francisco. The emperor's actual burial mound was a mortuary park enclosed by a wall three miles long. The tomb mound itself is easily more than the size of three football fields laid side by side and its central point is over 140 feet—or fourteen stories—high. Apparently it took years to create the mausoleum tomb with an estimated number of seven hundred thousand workers, many of whom must have been either prisoners or in forced labor, some of whom we are told were first castrated. Four great pits surround the as-yet unexcavated imperial tomb. The tomb was said by the historian Sima Qian to have been constructed with liquid mercury rivers flowing—as replicated rivers of China—from the center. This remnant mercury in the actual tomb has impeded full excavation, since it is toxic. Each of the four pits covers a large space, some many acres, roughly 640 feet long and almost 200 feet wide, and inside three of the pits were the thousands of ceramic warriors. In Pit 1 the warriors are lined up in arrangements that suggest eleven trenches running side by side, each mostly about ten feet wide, but the others are not as easy to define spatially. The floors of the trenches were paved in brick and a wooden roof covered each pit. The huge tomb was probably begun early in Qin Shihuangdi's reign and may have taken forty years to fully build. Unfortunately, his offspring—his immediate successors—were unable to maintain his empire and it was broken up by 206 BC, after only half a century. The detailed records of Sima Qian (around 100 BC), whom later Chinese authorities call the Grand Historian, verify some of the tomb plans:

He had over 700,000 men transported to the spot . . . when he began digging and shaping Mt. Li . . . Replicas of palaces, scenic towers . . . as well as rare utensils and wonderful objects were brought to fill up the tomb. Craftsmen were ordered to set up crossbows and arrows, rigged so they would immediately shoot anyone attempting to break in. Mercury was used to fashion imitations of the hundred rivers, the Yellow River and the Yangtze, and the seas, constructed in such a way that they seemed to flow.

For comparison, no complete ancient public cemetery—let alone a private tomb complex—from the Western world of comparable vintage has yielded a fraction of the funerary objects or materials this single great mausoleum has preserved so well. For sheer size, not even the great Mausoleum of Halicarnassus came close. Halicarnassus's monument was one of the Seven Wonders of the Ancient World when constructed around 350 BC in Caria as a monument glorifying Mausolos, satrap of a Persian province, but it barely achieved one-quarter of this Chinese tomb's size.

This mausoleum contains the greatest single tomb artifact assemblage in the world

The number of buried artifacts in the great mausoleum—not yet even fully excavated—exceeds that of any other tomb assemblage in the world, already almost 20,000 individual objects, and the total number of artifacts may eventually be twice that, based on the volume of space still untouched. Pit 1 alone contains ranks of 3,210 ceramic infantrymen. Pit 2 contains more than 1,400 warriors and horses and about 1,400 bronze arrowheads along with at least 64 chariots and armored cavalry. Pit 3 is the smallest underground chamber and contains only about 70 warriors, apparently mostly officers, along with several bronze war chariots. The projected total of 7,000 to 8,000 ceramic warriors is complemented by hundreds of ceramic horses and almost 10,000 metal artifacts, many made of bronze and other alloyed metals.

The objects are in excellent condition

Although Xi'an has a temperate climate with regular rainfall and fairly high humidity, because most of the material found here is ceramic, it is in a remarkable state of preservation. This is partly because it was buried fairly deeply below surface moisture— around thirteen feet on average—in a landscape that was apparently altered for drainage purposes. Another reason the materials survived well is that the ceramic material was planned for a long existence. Even the bronze objects, including life-size imperial chariots with bronze horses and wheels, have been well preserved because of careful planning, so there is far less corrosion and oxidation than would be expected for a temperate climate with normal rainfall of fifty to seventy inches per year. Other metal objects have also survived well, and show much detail about remarkable Chinese metallurgy in the Qin dynasty. The ceramic (fired clay) figures themselves are largely intact although the painted colors have mostly faded away.

The ceramic—specifically, terra-cotta—statues of the thousands of warriors are made of the best possible material for mass production. Clay is used all over the world in sedentary, or agricultural, societies, and it is also usually found very close to where people have traditionally lived, near rivers where a volume of fresh water flowed. Clay itself is an erosional end product. The tiny clay particles start out as rock fragments, but after being driven along long rivers by water and gravity, the eroded material is worn down to fine grains after millions of years. The dual state of clay is also important here: before working, clay is malleable and can be formed into nearly any shape due to its water content, with water molecules surrounding the tiny clay particles. But after firing, when all the water is driven off, clay particles are fused together by vitrifying them in high temperature, making ceramic objects durable like stone. Because fired clay approaches the hardness of rock, vessels cannot easily disintegrate and are eventually in chemical equilibrium with the environment in which they are found. That is partly why the bulk of this gigantic tomb's objects, the ceramic figures of the warriors, can tell the world so much about their individual features—along with the culture that made them so lifelike—because they are in nearly perfect state.

The bronze of the war chariots and arrowheads also shows little corrosion, partly because the massive roof over each warrior pit was originally matted in woven patterns of vegetal rattanlike fiber and covered with fired clay, since fired clay is fairly impermeable to water. The tomb was designed to keep the artifacts as perfectly stable as possible for the longest imaginable time. Considering the excellent state of preservation, this plan apparently worked.

This tomb shows early Chinese technology at an earlier stage than previously known

In addition to what the giant tomb records about Chinese culture in the early dynastic period of the Qin, the technology they achieved at this time is staggering, far in advance of cultures in the West. For example, besides normal bronze (an alloy of copper and tin), other metals and alloys preserved in the tomb include copper-nickel, cobalt and even chromium. This advanced metallurgy dovetails perfectly with a Han dynasty record book dated only slightly later than the tomb. Chinese records also noted exact ratios for six kinds of bronze objects in copper and tin alloys, depending on the desired color and even chosen ringing sound, among other criteria. If you wanted a silvery color without paying the price for silver (always a clever ruse), Qin high-tin bronze would fool the eyes of most people from even a foot away. These metallurgical achievements may be some of the "wonderful objects" the historian Sima Qian recorded as being in the tomb.

The Chinese were certainly not the first to use an alloy of copper and tin for making bronze, but they achieved high-tin bronzes that the West never accomplished. Bronze usually contains 85 percent copper and 15 percent tin, but early Chinese bronze often has a tin portion of up to 22 percent. Since the melting temperature of copper is around 1984°F and that of tin about 450°F, it is easy to see why so little tin would be left in this ratio as it would have long burned away at the high temperature required to melt copper. New studies of Chinese bronze making suggest the metalworkers first poured and enclosed the molten tin in a circular crucible with a long neck, then poured the molten copper over it without allowing the tin to completely vaporize into gas and escape out of the crucible. This alloy process, apparently unheard of in the West, allowed such a durable bronze to look like silver and yet be much stronger.

From the smaller officers' pit of the mausoleum, seventeen completely intact swords, still sharp and shiny, were excavated. These were also very finely coated with a thin layer of chromium plating. Because this seems impossible, many metallurgists think this chromium plating was possibly accidental from the intense burning of some of the partly looted tomb pits, depositing chromium oxide on the bronze in a carbon-reducing atmosphere underground. Others are less sure, suggesting Chinese metallurgy was so advanced that this was a deliberate technology.

In addition, the melting temperatures of nickel, cobalt and chromium—needed for the Chinese alloys found in this tomb—are very high, higher than was commonly possible in the West until the Industrial Revolution. These very same metals weren't even discovered in the West until the mid eighteenth century, although some of them can occur naturally, usually in very small increments, with copper ore. Regardless, such an array of metallic materials begin to demonstrate the remarkable technology of ancient China, now better understood from this great tomb complex than from any other archaeological context.

So far over ten thousand bronze weapons have been excavated from the mausoleum. It is likely that each ceramic soldier held or had these real weapons close at hand. These weapons alone could outfit an army, which may be why some of the tomb's giant pits were robbed in 206 BC. They include spears, axes, pikes, daggers, swords, billhooks (long curved hooks used to snag, pierce and hold enemies for closer killing), crossbow triggers and arrowheads. Some of the arrowheads are chillingly deadly because they are alloyed with a toxic lead content. Their extra weight would give them stronger impact and greater killing power as projectiles from a crossbow—itself an advanced weapon for the day and not known in the West—as they would pierce deeper through armor and tissue. Perhaps they were even meant to cause lead poisoning if the victims could not remove them, although it is unknown if Chinese medicine recognized the effects of lead poisoning. Nonetheless, these are extremely advanced war technologies for around 200 BC and show how serious the Qin dynasty was about establishing and keeping the empire under tight control.

The clay warriors are amazingly detailed with individual features

Many are still skeptical that the facial features of each ceramic warrior seem to represent a unique individual, but this is nearly the case. Ethnic characteristics of many Chinese regions seem combined in these terra-cotta warriors, and this is multiplied by the variations in hair shape, ear shape, mustache length and direction and martial uniform as well as original color patterns. On the one hand, the regional variations account for about ten ethnic types; on the other hand, combinations are also evident: the round faces of the south are sometimes mixed with the long faces of the north, just as the eye shapes vary widely from east to west. The clever arrangement of these varied types is so compelling that no group of any twenty to thirty ceramic soldiers has the same ethnic and hair variations twice. There is still some debate that each face is an individual portrait, and even many Chinese scholars maintain this, but the more sensible explanation is that the facial types and their variations were designed to represent the ten or so regional ethnic groups that made up China in the perceptions of its people of the time.

. In their construction, the hollow ceramic heads of the warrior statues were attached to molded necks. There is far less variety in each hollow torso, all also made of standardized shapes over solid ceramic waists and legs. The bodies probably show less variation because they represented an army outfitted with government-issue uniforms, with also more regularity in featureless legs and feet sizes, although footgear differs. Even though intellectual individualism was suppressed at this time—perhaps setting a cultural tradition—there may be a philosophic statement here about the nature of imperial unity. Since unity actually implies multiple entities combined—hence the seemingly infinite individual faces which would occur in nature—this would serve one deliberate directive or common purpose, in this case military cohesion under the emperor.

The warriors' uniforms vary between ceramic versions of cotton padded armor and mail. They are almost all hatless or without headgear, but their stances are divided between cavalry on horses, infantry made up of foot soldiers, kneeling archers, spearmen and officers, among others. Two basic separate color schemes can be seen in Pit 1, one battle type dressed in black armor, with green coats and blue trousers, and the other group dressed in red armor with orange buttons.

The ceramic figures' heights are slightly staggered so that one almost never sees three adjacent soldiers of the exact same height. On the other hand, the average sizes of these ceramic figures are well over the average Chinese height in both ancient and modern history. Many are over six feet tall and some of the most important officers reach six feet, four inches. The emperor apparently wanted to proudly display a remarkable fighting force guarding his tomb, so that the seven to eight thousand warriors could be easily intimidating, both to the world they represented as well as in an afterlife. No other tomb in the world known to date has ever contained so many carefully constructed individual guards who represent such a high standard of craftsmanship. It is also unlikely that a similar number and variety of mausoleum guards will be found anywhere else, although China might yet yield additional surprises.

This site has stimulated archaeology in China more than any other site

Modern archaeology in China is a rigorous discipline, as practiced globally, but it must also be economically responsible by promoting tourism. China's bureaucrats and politicians hold state archaeologists to the highest standards, so there is often less room for flexibility in field methods, and excavation or publishing schedules are tightly regulated, unlike in the West, where some archaeologists never publish their field results. This would not be easily tolerated in modern China because of a political hierarchy that closely regulates archaeological research and controls all funding accordingly. When I met the excavator and curator of the Tomb of 10,000 Warriors at Stanford this past year, I was also introduced to bureaucrat-politicians who have equal or more say in matters of archaeological research. Continuing archaeological work, reported on in the summer of 2007, shows a massive 30-meter-high mystery structure with multiple staircases in the center of the mausoleum complex, which further research will certainly elucidate.

Because of the tomb's archaeological importance to tourism from outside China, typically the West, as well as tourism from inside China, travelers can now either fly directly into Xi'an, a major air hub of central China, or take the Qinghai-Tibet railway, newly finished in 2006, that runs from Beijing to Lhasa over the Tibetan Plateau directly through Xi'an. This is no accident, since archaeological tourism has grown exponentially since the wider publication of this tomb's results in the 1990s. Tour companies all over the world list this site as one of the "must-see" places in China, and it is certainly one of the top three visitor sights along with the Forbidden City of Beijing and the Great Wall. Now thousands of tourists from many countries visit the tomb nearly every day of the year. The staggering size and quantity of objects—especially the soldiers—in the tomb is indeed stunning, as well as functioning as archaeological proof underscoring the formidable power and deserved fearsome reputation of Qin Shihuangdi as China's first emperor. In *Eyewitness to Discovery* (1996), Brian Fagan confirms how important the tomb is to archaeology, and not just in China: "We can confidently expect that Shihuangdi's tomb to be one of the most spectacular excavations of the twenty-first century." Chinese archaeologists would hardly disagree.

The tomb provides details not previously known, such as martial arts history

Some of the ceramic warriors are in what is usually interpreted as a martial arts stance with tightly crooked arms, stiffened flat hands and forward-bent knees. We already know that hands-only martial arts originally developed out of Asia as a military discipline accompanied by a focused mental state with high concentration and toughened pain endurance. This martial arts tradition was possibly created after the sixth century BC from the philosophy of Sun Zi (Sun Tzu), who wrote *The Art of War*, although no clear history of martial arts existed until after AD 200. Because their stiffened hands are too tightly clenched, with their thumbs protected inside, these individual tomb warriors cannot be construed as holding anything in their hands, certainly not archers once holding bows as some maintain, so it is hard to interpret them in any other way than as martial arts experts of around 200 BC, making this the earliest evidence to date for martial arts combatants.

It helps us understand why the Han dynasty followed this first unification of China

The great Han dynasty (roughly 200 BC to AD 200) used to be considered a mystery arising out of the chaos of the Warring States period. In part because of imperial mandates seen even in this massive private tomb, now the beginning of the Han dynasty in China is no longer a shadowy period with more questions than answers. However short-lived its dynasty, the Qin Tomb of 10,000 Warriors—one that so manifested the unprecedented power of its emperor—made it obviously apparent to the next generations, the Han dynasty, that China could be unified into a centralized empire. This happened again and again in Chinese history, partly based on the model of Qin Shihuangdi's immense state reorganization and enormous imperial bureaucracy.

Later emperors could learn from Qin Shihuangdi, and even the much later mandarins could understand what it would take to run a vast country like China. Following his example they rationalized their sometimes brutal control of large populations and resources. Values and virtues could be taught over generations to slowly mold a diverse population into a workforce that would turn out the finest ceramics, metals and textiles both the ancient and the modern world would ever see. Such a workforce could also produce an agricultural bounty through careful planning and requisitioning. State support could nurture craftspeople who would develop innovative and lucrative imperial industries. Centralized government has always had its terrible weaknesses, usually at the cost of colorful regionalism and even more often at the expense of individualism. On the other hand, China's long history frequently showcases the strengths of wisely administered centralization, begun under Qin Shihuangdi over two thousand years ago. Where would the West be without China's inventive genius in silk, fine bone china and porcelain; where would Western technology be without gunpowder or paper inked with typescript or credit currencies that foreshadowed modern currencies? These were all carefully controlled state and imperial crafts. Marco Polo's astonishment at Chinese technology and conquest in the Khan period and at the wonders of the Yuan dynasty is understandable. After seeing the massive Xi'an mausoleum, these technologies are now more understandable in light of the vast numbers of people who were controlled under a ruthless regime seeking the widest production of goods for state and imperial benefit, a pattern started under the unification of the first true emperor, Qin Shihuangdi, around 221 BC.

Conclusion

The Tomb of 10,000 Warriors was (and still is) not only a poetic equation representing imperial strength—its "uncountable" guards stretching to the horizon of the tomb's underground pits—but it was also a prediction of China's future. Here, without any known precedent, the first emperor of China, Qin Shihuangdi, achieved the marvelous amalgamation of China's most important resource—its population. These thousands of individual ceramic warrior faces over a standardized set of uniforms and highly organized military regimentation are somehow a philosophic statement of a unity achieved at great cost, but also one with great state potential, redirecting the individual to empower the state. Perhaps this is one of many possible reasons that modern China has paradoxically imbibed the best of both Marxism and Capitalism while still maintaining the philosophic legacy of Emperor Qin Shihuangdi. This emperor and his tomb changed perceptions in both ancient and modern China as well as the world at large, but his tomb connects the present to the past with an astonishing statement of power.

Selected Bibliography

GENERAL

Atwood, Roger. *Stealing History: Tomb Raiders, Smugglers and Looting of the Ancient World*. New York: St. Martin's Press, 2004.

Bahn, Paul. *Lost Treasures: Great Discoveries in World Archaeology*. New York: Barnes and Noble, 2000.

Ceram, C. W. *Gods, Graves, Scholars: The Story of Archaeology*. 2nd rev. ed. New York: Random House Value Publishing, 1994.

Fagan, Brian. *Quest for the Past: Great Discoveries in Archaeology*. 2nd ed. Long Grove, Ill.: Waveland Press, 1994.

————, ed. *The Oxford Companion to Archaeology*. Oxford: Oxford University Press, 1996.

Palmer, Douglas, with Paul Bahn and Joyce Tyldesley. *Unearthing the Past*. Guilford, Conn.: The Lyons Press, 2005.

Reeves, Nicholas. *Ancient Egypt: The Great Discoveries*. London: Thames and Hudson, 2000.

Renfrew, Colin. *Virtual Archaeology: Great Discoveries Brought to Life Through Virtual Reality*. London: Thames and Hudson, 1997.

Robbins, Lawrence. *Stones, Bones and Ancient Cities: Great Discoveries in Archaeology*. New York: St. Martin's Press, 1990.

Romer, J., and E. Romer. *Great Excavations: John Romer's History of Archaeology*. London: Cassell, 2000.

Scarre, Christopher, ed. *The Seventy Wonders of the Ancient World: The Great Monuments and How They Were Built*. London: Thames and Hudson, 1999.

ROSETTA STONE

Andrews, Carol. *The British Museum Book of the Rosetta Stone*. London: British Museum Press, 1986.

Baines, John, and Jaromir Malek. *Cultural Atlas of Ancient Egypt*. New York: Checkmark Books, 2000.

Davies, W. V. *Egyptian Hieroglyphs: Reading the Past*. London: British Museum Press, 1987.

Fagan, Brian. *The Rape of the Nile: Tomb Robbers, Tourists, and Archaeologists in Egypt*. Rev. ed. Boulder, Colo.: Westview Press, 2004.

Hirst, Anthony, and M. S. Silk, eds. *Alexandria, Real and Imagined*. Center for Hellenic Studies, King's College London. London: Asgate Publishing, 2004.

James, T. G. H. *The British Museum Concise Introduction to Ancient Egypt*. Ann Arbor: University of Michigan Press, 2005.

Parkinson, Richard. *Cracking Codes: The Rosetta Stone and Decipherment*. London: British Museum Press; Berkeley: University of California Press, 1999.

Reeves, Nicholas. *Ancient Egypt: The Great Discoveries*. London: Thames and Hudson, 2000.

Robinson, Andrew. *The Story of Writing*. London: Thames and Hudson, 1995. Ch. 1, "Reading the Rosetta Stone," 20–35.

Vercoutter, Jean. *The Search for Ancient Egypt*. New York: Harry Abrams, 1992.

TROY

Brackman, Arnold. *The Dream of Troy*. New York: Van Nostrand Reinhold, 1979.

Cline, Eric H. *Sailing the Wine-Dark Sea: International Trade and the Bronze Age Aegean*. (BAR) British Archaeological Reports—International Series 594. Oxford: Tempus Reparatum, 1994.

Easton, Donald. *Schliemann's Excavations at Troia 1870–1873*. Munich: Philip von Zabern, 2002.

Jablonka, Peter, and C. Brian Rose. "Late Bronze Age Troy: A Response to Frank Kolb." *American Journal of Archaeology* 108, no. 4 (October, 2004).

Korfmann, Manfred. *Studia Troica* 1–10. Mainz: Philip von Zabern, 1991–2000.

Latacz, Joachim. *Troy and Homer: Towards a Solution of an Old Mystery*. Translated by K. Windle. Oxford: Oxford University Press, 2005.

Mellink, Machteld, ed. *Troy and the Trojan War*. Bryn Mawr Troy Symposium 1984. Bryn Mawr: Bryn Mawr College, 1986.

Ottaway, James. "New Assault on Troy." *Archaeology* 44 (1991): 54–59.

Traill, David. *Schliemann of Troy: Treasure and Deceit*. 1995. Reprint, New York: Penguin, 2000.

Wood, Michael. *In Search of the Trojan War*. 1985. Reprint, London: BBC Books, 2005.

NINEVEH AND THE ASSYRIAN LIBRARY

Collon, Dominique, and Andrew George, eds. *Nineveh: Papers of the XLIXe Recontre Assyriologique Internationale, London (2003)*. London: British School of Archaeology in Iraq, 2005.

Dalley, Stephanie. "Nineveh, Babylon and the Hanging Gardens: Cuneiform and Classical Sources Reconciled." *Iraq* (Journal of the British School of Archaeology in Iraq) 56 (1994): 45–58.

Finkel, Irving. "The Hanging Gardens of Babylon." In *Seven Wonders of the Ancient World*, edited by Martin Price, London: Routledge, 1981.

Layard, Austen Henry. *Nineveh and Its Remains*. London: John Murray, 1854. Facsimile, Elibron Classics/Adamant, 2001.

Reade, Julian. *Assyrian Sculpture*. London: British Museum Press, 1983.

Russell, John Malcolm. *Sennacherib's "Palace without Rival" at Nineveh*. Chicago: University of Chicago Press, 1992.

Saggs, H. W. F. *The Might That Was Assyria*. London: Sidgwick and Jackson, 1984.

Scott, M. Louise, and John MacGinnis. "Notes on Nineveh." *Iraq* (Journal of British School of Archaeology in Iraq) 52 (1990): 63–73.

Silverberg, Robert. *The Man Who Found Nineveh: The Story of Austen Henry Layard*. New York: Holt, Rinehart & Winston, 1964.

Stronach, David, and Steven Lumsden. "U.C. Berkeley's Excavations at Nineveh." *Biblical Archaeologist* 55 (1992): 227–33.

KING TUT'S TOMB

Bierbrier, Morris L. *The Tomb Builders of the Pharaohs*. New York: Scribner, 1985.

Carter, Howard, and A. C. Mace. *The Discovery of the Tomb of Tutankhamen*. Reprint, New York: Dover Publications, 1977.

———. *The Tomb of Tut-Ankh-Amen: Discovered by the Late Earl of Carnarvon and Howard Carter*. 1923. Reprint, London: Duckworth, 2003.

Fletcher, Joann, et al. *Who Killed King Tut?: Using Modern Forensics to Solve a 3300-Year-Old Mystery*. Amherst, NY: Prometheus Books, 2004.

Freed, Rita, Yvonne Markowitz, and Sue D'Auria, eds. *Pharaohs of the Sun: Akhenaten, Nefertiti, Tutankhamen*. Boston: Museum of Fine Arts, 1999.

Hawass, Zawi. *Tutankhamun and the Golden Age of the Pharaohs: Official Companion Book to the Exhibition sponsored by National Geographic*. Washington, DC: National Geographic, 2005.

James, T. G. H. *Howard Carter: The Path to Tutankhamen*. London: Tauris Park, 2001.

El Mahdy, Christine. *Tutankhamen: The Life and Death of a Boy-King*. New York: St. Martin's Press, 1999.

Reeves, Nicholas. *The Complete Tutankhamun: The King, the Tomb, the Royal Treasure*. 1990. Reprint, London: Thames and Hudson, 1995.

———. *Ancient Egypt: The Great Discoveries*. London: Thames and Hudson, 2000.

MACHU PICCHU

Bingham, Alfred. *Machu Picchu: Portrait of Hiram Bingham*. Boston: Abeel Publishers, 2000.

Bingham, Hiram. *Lost City of the Incas: The Story of Machu Picchu and Its Builders*. 1948. Reprint, Westport, CT: Greenwood Press, 1981.

———. *Inca Land: Explorations in the Highlands of Peru*. National Geographic Adventure Classics. Washington, DC: National Geographic Press, 2003.

Burger, Richard, and Lucy Salazar, eds. *Machu Picchu: Unveiling the Mystery of the Incas*. New Haven: Yale University Press, 2004.

Hagen, Victor W. von. *The Incas: People of the Sun*. New York: Collins World, 1977.

Hemming, John. *Machu Picchu*. Wonders of Man. New York: Newsweek Books, 1981.

————. *The Conquest of the Incas*. New York: Harvest/Harcourt, 2003.

Lewin, Ted. *Lost City: The Discovery of Machu Picchu*. New York: Philomel/Penguin, 2003.

Moseley, Michael. *The Incas and Their Ancestors*. London: Thames and Hudson, 1992.

Wright, Kenneth, Alfredo Zegarra, Ruth Wright, and Gordon MacEwan. *Machu Picchu: A Civil Engineering Marvel*. American Society of Civil Engineers, 2000.

POMPEII

Ciarello, Annamaria. *Gardens of Pompeii*. Rome: L'Erma di Bretschneider, 2000.

Etienne, Robert. *The Day a City Died*. New York: New Discoveries, Thames and Hudson, 1992.

Grant, Michael. *Eros in Pompeii: The Secret Rooms of the National Museum of Naples*. New York: William Morrow, 1975.

Jenkins, Ian, and Kim Sloan. *Vases and Volcanoes: Sir William Hamilton and His Collection*. London: British Museum Press, 1996.

Laurence, Ray. *Roman Pompeii*. London: Routledge, 1996.

Ranieri Panetta, Marisa. *Pompeii: The History, Life and Art of the Buried City*. White Star Press, 2004.

Sontag, Susan. *The Volcano Lover*. 1992. Reprint, New York: Picador, 2004.

Varone, Antonio, and Eric Lessing. *Pompeii*. New York: Terrail, 1997.

Wallace-Hadrill, Andrew. *Houses and Society in Pompeii and Herculaneum*. Princeton: Princeton University Press, 1996.

Zanker, Paul. *Pompeii: Public and Private Life*. Translated by D. L. Schneider. Revealing Antiquity Series, vol 11. Cambridge, Mass.: Harvard University Press, 1998.

DEAD SEA SCROLLS

Abegg, Martin G., and Peter Flint. *The Dead Sea Scrolls Bible: The Oldest Known Bible Translated for the First Time into English*. New York: HarperCollins, 1999.

Charlesworth, James. *Jesus and the Dead Sea Scrolls*. Anchor Bible Reference Library. New York: Random House, 2006.

Davies, Philip, George Brooke, and Phillip Callaway. *The Complete World of the Dead Sea Scrolls*. London: Thames and Hudson, 2002.

Eisenman, Robert H., and Michael Wise. *The Dead Sea Scrolls Uncovered: 50 Key Documents Withheld for Over 35 Years*. New York: Penguin, 1993.

Flint, Peter. *The Dead Sea Scrolls: An Essential Guide*. New York: Abingdon Press, 2007.

Hirschfeld, Yizhar. *Qumran in Context: Reassessing the Archaeological Evidence*. Peabody, MA: Hendrickson Publishers, 2004.

Schiffman, Lawrence. *Reclaiming the Dead Sea Scrolls*. Anchor Bible Reference Library. New York: Random House, 1995.

Schuller, Eileen. *The Dead Sea Scrolls: What Have We Learned?* Louisville, Ky.: Westminster/John Knox Press, 2006.

Vanderkam, James, and Peter Flint. *The Meaning of the Dead Sea Scrolls: Their Significance for Understanding the Bible, Judaism, Jesus and Christianity*. Reprint, San Francisco: HarperSanFrancisco, 2004.

Vermes, Geza, ed. and trans. *The Complete Dead Sea Scrolls in English*. 1962. Rev. ed. New York: Penguin, 2004.

AKROTIRI AT THERA

Casson, Lionel. *The Ancient Mariners*. 2nd ed. Princeton: Princeton University Press, 1991.

Cline, Eric H. *Sailing the Wine-Dark Sea: International Trade and the Late Bronze Age Aegean*. BAR-International Series 591. Oxford: Tempus Reparatum, 1994.

Doumas, Christos. *Thera: Pompeii of the Ancient Aegean: Excavations at Akrotiri 1967–1979*. London: Thames and Hudson, 1983.

Forsyth, Phyllis Young. *Thera in the Bronze Age*. American University Studies IX: History. New York: Peter Lang Publishing, 1999.

Manning, Sturt. *A Test of Time: The Volcano of Thera and the Chronology and History of the Aegean and East Mediterranean in the Mid Second Millennium BC*. Oxford: Oxbow Books, 1999.

Marinatos, Nanno. "Thera." In *An Encyclopedia of the History of Classical Archaeology* (L–Z), edited by Nancy Thomson de Grummond, 1097–98. Westport, CT: Greenwood Press, 1996.

Marinatos, Spyridon. *Excavations at Thera 1–7*. Athens: Greek Archaeological Service, 1967–76.

Palyvou, Clairy. *Akrotiri, Thera: An Architecture of Affluence 3,500 Years Old*. Prehistory Monographs 15. Philadelphia, Pa.: INSTAP (Institute for Aegean Prehistory) Academic Press, 2005.

Pellegrino, Charles. *Unearthing Atlantis: An Archaeological Odyssey to the Fabled Lost Civilization*. New York: HarperCollins, 1991.

Shelmerdine, Cynthia, ed. *The Cambridge Companion to the Aegean Bronze Age*. Cambridge: Cambridge University Press, 1994.

OLDUVAI GORGE

Isaac, Glynn Llywelyn, ed. *Human Origins: Louis Leakey and the East African Evidence (Perspectives on Human Evolution)*. W. A. Benjamin, 1976.

Johanson, Donald, and Maitland Edey. *Lucy: The Beginnings of Humankind*. New York: Touchstone Books, 1981.

Johanson, Donald, with Blake Edgar. *From Lucy to Language*. New York: Simon & Schuster, 1996.

Klein, Richard. *The Dawn of Human Culture*. New York: Wiley, 2002.

Leakey, Mary D. *Olduvai Gorge: My Search for Early Man*. New York: Collins, 1979.

Morrell, Virginia. *Ancestral Passions: The Leakey Family and the Quest for Humankind's Beginnings*. New York: Touchstone Books, 1995.

Schick, Kathy D., and Nicholas Toth. *Making Silent Stones Speak: Human Evolution and the Dawn of Technology*. Trafalgar Square, 1994.

TOMB OF 10,000 WARRIORS

Fu Tianchou, ed. *Wonders from the Earth: The First Emperor's Underground Army*. Rev. ed. San Francisco: China Books and Periodicals, 1989.

Giusso, R. W. L., and Catherine Pagani with David Miller. *The First Emperor of China*. New York: Birch Lane Press, 1989.

Ho, Erling. "China's Great Enigma: What's Inside the Unexcavated Tomb of Emperor Shihuangdi?" *Archaeology* 54, no. 5 (September/ October 2001).

Klein, Julia. "The Rise of China." *Archaeology* 59, no. 4 (July/August 2006).

Kwang-Chih Chang et al. (Sarah Allan, Ping Fang Xu, Liancheng Lu and Wangping Shao). *The Formation of Chinese Civilization: An Archaeological Perspective*. New Haven: Yale University Press/New World Press, 2002.

Li Liu and Xingcan Chen. *State Formation in Early China*. Duckworth Debates in Archaeology. London: Duckworth Publishing, 2003.

Sima Qian. *Records of the Grand Historian: Qin Dynasty*. Translated by Burton Watson. Renditions. New York: Columbia University Press; Chinese University of Hong Kong, 1993.

Xiaoneng Yang, ed. *New Perspectives on China's Past: Twentieth-Century Chinese Archaeology*. New Haven: Yale University Press/Nelson Atkins Museum of Art, 2004.

———, ed. *The Golden Age of Chinese Archaeology: Celebrated Discoveries from The People's Republic of China*. Washington, DC: National Gallery, 1999. Esp. pp. 366–87.

Yuan Zhongyi. *Terra Cotta Warriors*. Beijing: People's China Publishing House, 1996.